BOTH THINGS ARE TRUE

A Journey from Fearing Trust to Trusting Fear

JANINE VALENTINE

Both Things Are True: A Journey from Fearing Trust to Trusting Fear
Published by Cairn Publishers LLC
Denver, CO

ISBN: 978-0-578-36705-7
Personal growth

Cover design by Jenn Valentine, copyright owned by Janine Valentine.
Interior design by Victoria Wolf, wolfdesignandmarketing.com, copyright owned by Janine Valentine.
Back photo by Julie Nelson.

PUBLISHERS

For the Wendies and Lo,
my core tribe.
To be seen, known, and loved
Is beauty beyond measure.

To Fear—
Thank you.

PREFACE

MARCH 2020 HIT THE WORLD like a gut punch. We were all trauma-tized on some level by the onset of the COVID-19 pandemic. We experienced isolation, both global and individual. There was fear. We felt powerless. The topic of vulnerability had been in vogue the previous few years, largely due to the powerful work of Brené Brown. It hit home in new ways during this time. I remember believing that vulnerability was something I could choose … something I wanted to consciously choose more often and practice in safe spaces. But the truth is that sometimes vulnerability chooses us.

We tend to think of things that scare us as things that happen to other people, not us. We empathize with others' situations while keeping them on the periphery of our personal reality, perhaps needing to believe it could not happen to us. This is not a conscious effort; we cannot walk around overiden-tifying with all the pain in the world. Then something scary happens to us, and we become aware that it never occurred to us that this thing could be our own reality rather than something we read about happening somewhere else, to someone else. We are someone else. They are us. We are humanity.

One. This pandemic was happening to all of us. We all began to find ourselves perhaps a bit more vulnerable than we would have chosen, and certainly for longer than we wanted.

A year and half into our new COVID world, in an attempt to begin to normalize this new way of being, I took a carefully planned vacation with a group of my friends across several international borders. We did all the things we had to do to travel: polymerase chain reaction (PCR) tests before flying out, wearing masks for thirty-eight hours of airline travel and airport layovers, and lots of extra electronic paperwork for each country we flew through—showing our vaccinations, and PCR test results, and proof of our reservations at our destination—along with our passports. It was an exhausting journey, but well worth it to finally go somewhere. I had a spectacular vacation, but this story begins on the second-to-last day of that vacation, when we all took yet another PCR test in order to travel home. This time, I tested positive. My travel companions all had to fly home without me, leaving me on the other side of the world to quarantine on my own without resources or cash, with no plan in place for my care, and about to be sick with COVID. This was a whole new level of vulnerability, isolation, fear, and powerlessness. I met myself there. I met God there.

I will use the terms God, Universe, and Source interchangeably throughout this book. I also capitalize "Sea" when I speak of my conversations with the Sea, because those were God-conscious conversations. This book is not about religion or how anyone refers to their higher power. It is about trust and fear and truth and doubt. It is about community and aloneness. It is about healing.

This is my very personal story, and yet it is about all of us. This was written for me, and for you. I knew very early into the experience that I would write about this. The details of our experiences are certainly unique, but the *experience* of our experiences is not. My journey and circumstances look different than yours, and yet each of us goes through things that test us and push us way outside our comfort zones, things that force us to face our worst fears and change us forever. We all have fears. We all have that one thing that we fear more than any other. And, in my experience, we will each be invited, and often forced, to face that very worst fear head-on at some point in our lives. If you are like me, just hearing that makes you cringe in … well, fear. My Big Fear was of being alone. I was triggered by anything that made me feel abandoned, not chosen, or like I did not belong. It wasn't just about physical aloneness; it was about psychological and spiritual aloneness. I faced this Big Fear for the first time when my husband and I divorced after nearly thirty years of marriage and I moved to an apartment to live alone for the first time in my life at the age of forty-eight. It turned out that this was just step one. I did learn to love living alone over the next seven years and even became genuinely grateful for the divorce that set me free to find and express my true self. And, as we know, life is all about layers. In hindsight, of course there was another layer on this journey to release my Big Fear. For me, step two came unexpectedly in the Maldives in September 2021.

Going through these traumatic events that force us to face our Big Fears is how we expand into who we truly are, who we were before we built our defense systems and believed the voices of others (and the voice in our own heads) about who or how we are in this world—often ignoring what our soul tells us. I believe this story will be deeply relatable—if not for you *yet*, it likely will be *someday*. Because this scary, hard stuff is going to happen to all of us. It is why we all feel it in our gut in the movie *Taken* when Liam Neeson's character tells his daughter, who is hiding under the bed, that she is going to be taken. The thing is, you are going to be taken. I was taken. We will all be taken at some point in our lives by the very things we fear. It is unavoidable. The things we fear will eventually have us because they are happening for us. I have been profoundly changed by this experience, and my prayer is that this is a healing balm for some of you reading this, as well as a toolbox of sorts for those of you who perhaps will be taken by your Big Fear sometime after reading this.

I pulled directly from the journal I kept while in quarantine, sharing my story as it actually was, the moment-by-moment truth of who and how I was, unpolished and real. The rest of the book was written in the four months immediately after my return home while the emotions were still on the surface and my body still held the physical memories. It is raw, vulnerable, and emotional. There are a few ugly moments and certainly some embarrassing ones, and I left them all in. They are all necessary to show my journey from resistance and fear to surrender and growth. There are surprisingly humorous moments. (And yes, it is absolutely okay to laugh at me as well as with me. It is not too soon. Trust me, the funny parts are already funny even to me.) I also share with you the unexpectedly glorious beauty in my ashes. This is an experience I do not wish on anyone, *and* I am already eternally grateful for it. Because truly, both things are true.

Writing this required extra self-care, focused self-awareness, and lots of self-love and compassion. It was a very cathartic and internal process. I sought out Reiki every few weeks to keep myself open, burned through dozens of candles, and took more baths and showers than I can count because my body needed to be in water to self-soothe and release after each writing session. I received a vision in one of my Reiki sessions in which I was sitting on a hill under a beautiful blue sky when suddenly hundreds of pink flower petals rained down on me—just directly over me—and into a basket I was holding. I understood that these were gifts from my angels and guides—downloads. I was not writing alone.

This is my story, and this is our story. It came to me, through me, for me … and also, for you.

DEPARTURE

I WOKE UP TO MY FINAL DAY OF VACATION on an exquisite boat out in the middle of the Indian Ocean. I had traveled with eleven of my friends, and we had just completed a week on ScubaSpa Yang, a fifty-meter luxury dive boat in the Maldives. I felt rested, relaxed, and sufficiently spoiled. I packed my small bag. I had needed only swimsuits and a few outfits to throw over a swimsuit for our seven days at sea. It was still dark. I liked watching the sunrise while drinking my coffee on deck. Rituals had been birthed in that past week, and I wanted to enjoy this experience one last time. So I wandered out to the deck and sat by myself while I watched the slow perfection of yet another sunrise. Shahadat, the bartender from Bangladesh who memorized every guest's perfect morning beverage and simply made it for each of us as soon as we showed up on deck, presented me with my dark black coffee. I am a purist when it comes to my coffee and my champagne; additions only detract from the deliciousness presented in their organic state. My friend and boat roommate, Wendy, joined me at the bar, and her cappuccino quietly appeared in front of her. A few other guests began trickling out of their rooms.

It was checkout day, so we were all taking our time packing in our rooms and then queueing up to pay our tabs.

Max, the boat manager, walked up to the bar and set a single sheet of paper in front of me. He had a look of concern on his face as he pointed to some typed print on the page. Uh-oh, did I order something ridiculously expensive and not know it? Oh well … it was worth it, whatever it was. This vacation was stellar. I followed Max's finger to where it rested on the page, pointing to one word: DETECTED. I was not sure what it meant.

"You have tested positive for COVID-19," he said.

What? Denial slammed into my body like a semitruck. I felt perfectly fine! I had no symptoms. My logical mind began a silent argument with the situation. I had only been on this boat, at sea, for the past week, around all the same people, and we were all negative for COVID when we arrived. And they were all still negative. This could not be correct.

The boat manager had brought a lab technician on board the day before to test all the guests to fulfill our requirement for flying home. Max explained to me that only one other guest tested positive, a woman from Russia with whom I had spent literally zero time. My roommate, Wendy, was negative, and our beds had been only a foot apart in our shared room. The Russian woman's husband was negative. The other ten friends I was traveling with were all negative. It was perplexing and felt unfair.

My thoughts began to spin faster than I could log them. Max continued speaking, telling Wendy that she could leave with me if she wanted to. Leave with me? Where was I going? He was still talking, unaware that I was inwardly freaking out. I looked at Max and told him I knew he was speaking, yet I could not grasp the specifics of the words. The bottom had dropped out from underneath me. I needed to go to my room so I would have the privacy to cry. Sob, really. I told Max I would return in a few minutes. I was scared. No, that's too mild. I was terrified. I knew what this meant.

I was about to be left behind— my greatest fear in the whole world.

I melted into my tears in the privacy of my room. I spoke my fear in quiet, disjointed gasps, wanting to swallow them whole before they could be witnessed, but they just bubbled up anyway. It was too much to hold inside like I normally would. My body could not contain the emotion this time. Wendy came into the room and held me tight and told me that she was going with me. I loved her so much for that. She had to be scared too, and it certainly was not how she expected to spend her last day in the Maldives before flying out that night. Yet she did not hesitate—not even one heartbeat. My whole body flooded with gratitude to not have to go through whatever was coming next alone.

Our whole group had talked about the possibility of this happening when we were planning our vacation. We had agreed that if one or more of us were to test positive for the return trip, we would need to leave them behind. We all had jobs to get back to; it would be a significant additional expense and hardship for any of us to stay as a companion to the person with COVID-19. Of course, at the time, it was a hypothetical. None of us believed it would actually happen. It certainly never occurred to me that I would be the one. The hypothetical situation that played like a movie in my mind was someone else in the group tested positive and I had to be one of the people leaving that person behind. The reality of this situation had not been fully contemplated by any of us. This was going to be so hard, for all of us. No one in our group of twelve would escape without some emotional scarring.

Wendy and I returned to deck with our suitcases in tow. I didn't even try to look like I hadn't been crying. My eyes were red and puffy and still leaking tears against my will. Max explained that the two of us were the first passengers who had ever tested positive on his boat. He said honestly that they didn't have a plan. Let me repeat that. They did not have a plan. This was not reassuring. He was not sure what was going to happen next, only that we were going to be taken off the boat by dinghy over to the city of Malé on the island of K.Malé. He would send a member of his deck crew, Shifaau, with us to get us to the clinic and interpret for us. Perhaps this was a false positive, so we would retest to be sure. I felt certain it must be a false positive … or at least I told myself that. Deep underneath, I think part of me was expecting the horrible corroboration of a second positive test. But I wasn't willing to follow that thought yet.

We sat on a bench at the very back of the boat, next to where we would board the dinghy, and waited for the Russian woman and her husband so we could head to the clinic. Tears continued to spill out in little waves. I just stared into space, wishing myself off this boat where people were starting to notice. Word was spreading. Understandably, most people did not want to come near me, so instead they overemphasized their concern with their body language—sad faces, hands to heart, or prayer hands. Oh hell, it was awful! These pantomimed motions of pity and fear were almost unbearable. They signaled our separation—a gaping chasm between the one who was contagious with a scary disease and those who were gratefully healthy.

One exception to this was my friend Robyn, who came right up to me when she saw that I was upset. When I told her not to get close because I was positive for COVID, she stepped closer, right next to me, and put one hand on my chest over my heart, and the other hand on my lower back. She just held them there and asked softly, "Are you scared?" I nodded yes. We stood in silence, her hands firmly on my heart and my back, for several more minutes. She gave me the gift of honesty, space to acknowledge what I was feeling, and the power of human touch. I was still scared, but I was calmer when she let go and stepped back.

Max offered us breakfast while we waited. It felt like such an odd suggestion. I was nauseated and could not possibly have eaten, but regardless, it would have been completely irresponsible for me to go into the dining room around other guests, not to mention serving myself from the buffet, after having just tested positive for COVID. Clearly, this truly was his first rodeo with this virus.

Wendy and I and the Russian couple boarded the dinghy around 8:00 a.m. I hadn't even had the chance to say goodbye to many of my friends and travel companions. As our little boat sped away, I looked back and immediately wished I had not. The crew and staff were out on the upper Thai deck, making more heart hands, prayer hands, hands to their chests, looks of sadness and fear and horror. I knew their intention. They all wished me well. Yet that snapshot would linger in my memory and haunt me, possibly for the rest of my life.

DAY ONE,
SEPTEMBER 25, 2021

THE DAY TECHNICALLY BEGAN a couple of hours earlier, but for me Day One of my experience (the part that I am writing about) began here with my arrival on the dock in the city of Malé. The other woman and her husband got off the boat. My friend got off the boat. Then it was my turn. I am five feet, two inches tall, and that first step up from the boat edge to the dock was shoulder height for me. The boat was bobbing up and down with the waves. I wanted to just crumple onto the floor of the boat. I was already doing a very hard thing, dammit! Why does just stepping off the boat have to be so hard in the midst of this? I could not do it alone. The Russian man reached down from above, while our guide steadied me on the rim of the boat edge. I breathed in sharply and pushed off in full fear, and also in full trust of the men who had hold of my hands, with everything I had in me. It wasn't pretty, but I was standing on the dock. Getting off the dinghy onto that dock was a metaphor foreshadowing my entire experience in quarantine.

The people on this island were conservative Muslims. The women were expected to cover everything but their eyes when out in public, even wearing gloves so their hands were not bare. The expectation was lowered for foreign women visiting, but the respectful thing to do was to keep our legs covered (at least over the knee, if not all the way to the ankle) and shoulders covered, no deep necklines, and no bare midriff. It was important that I complied the best I could. Standing on the dock above our dinghy, I put on a face mask and then donned my only long-sleeved shirt over my tank top. I was already wearing my capri-length pants, which were the only pants I had with me. Our little group then walked down the dock to the edge of the city. Our deck-crew-guy-turned-guide hailed two cabs for all of us, and we were taken down narrow and crowded streets to a building with lettering on the outside declaring it was the Tourist Inn. It did not look like a place that tourists would seek out. I thought we were going to the clinic. No one had explained what we were doing here.

We walked into the Tourist Inn and obediently followed our guide silently up three floors on a spiral staircase to a reception area. He spoke with the man behind the desk while the four of us just sat facing each other on hard wooden chairs in the small space next to the desk. After waiting about a half hour, we were told to follow the guy at the desk up another two floors of winding stairs. We went through a locked door, which he unlocked for us, into a common area that had a round table with four chairs and a kitchenette along the wall. There was a window, which was open. The traffic in the busy street below was loud with the constant beeps of moped horns, which sounded uncannily like bleating goats. There were four doors off this central room, one in each corner. Wendy and I were shown into one corner room, and the Russian couple into another corner room. We were to wait there until Shifaau, our interpreter from the boat, came to get us to go to the clinic for retesting.

The room was small. A king bed took up almost all of the floor space. There was just enough room to walk around the bed. Most notably, there were no windows. A big television on the wall played what looked like an Indian soap opera. There was no desk, but instead some sort of tiny vanity built into the wall with a ledge and a mirror. There was an ensuite bathroom; the toilet literally sat in the shower, and there was no door.

At 9:30 a.m. we got a call on the room phone to come downstairs. Shifaau was there waiting for us. We would walk to the clinic. We went single file because the streets were so narrow. Cars and mopeds were whipping past us. I felt the heat of their engines. More than one side mirror almost hit me. There were lots of pedestrians. We passed men sitting at little outside tables and benches, smoking and drinking coffee. There were several women in burkas doing their shopping at the fruit stands and markets. We were being stared at every step of the way. This was obviously not a touristed part of the island, and we stood out in the crowd. It may have just been that we were something unique to watch, but I was conscious that we, as women, were not dressed and covered appropriately. No one smiled at us. Their stares felt stern and disapproving.

We arrived at the little medical clinic. Three women in burkas behind the desk processed our paperwork. I paid nearly $200 USD to expedite the test results so they would come back in four hours rather than eight hours. Four hours would mean I could still make my flight out that night with my friends. Eight hours would mean I'd miss my flight even if I got a negative test back. I was still holding out hope. One of the women behind the desk pointed me to the back of the room where there was a row of metal chairs against the wall in what felt like the hallway. I took a seat in one of the chairs and was soon joined by the Russian woman from the boat, also finished with her paperwork. Another woman in a burka signaled for me to follow her through a doorway just off the hallway into an even smaller room. She motioned for me to remove my mask and open my mouth. She took a throat swab and then a nasal swab. Our eyes met. She had kind eyes. I teared up again at the shared humanity in this moment, and then put my mask back on and shuffled in a daze back out into the crowded streets to follow our leader back to what I was already referring to in my head as my holding cell.

Wendy and I watched Bollywood movies with subtitles and wished away the four hours of waiting. We got hungry and thirsty, but there was nothing in the room. We ventured down to the reception area where the man who checked us in was still sitting at his desk. We managed to figure out that he did not have any snacks or water he could sell to us, but he could exchange our US dollars for Maldivian Rufiyaa to go shopping with. Another guest walked through the reception area in this moment, and thankfully his English was better. He was able to tell us there was a little market across the street to the right when we exited the building. We took our colorful Maldivian paper money and wound our way down the stairs to the street level. Sure enough, there on the right exactly as promised was a tiny market. It was like shopping at a gas station in the US, similar both in size and selection. We did find the chocolate puff cookies we had both enjoyed with our coffee every morning on the boat and had a tiny celebration in the store aisle at the familiarity of them. We bought the cookies along with a can of what looked like Pringles potato chips except they were purple, a small bag of trail mix with nuts and dried fruit, and bottled waters. The man rang us up, and we were eleven Rufiyaa short (about a dollar in US funds). As we began deciding which item to remove from the bag, the man said in English, "You bring later," motioning us out the door. The kindness of a stranger, willing to trust us to return with the money, was reassuring to my soul in all the chaos and distrustful energy of this day.

We returned to our room, sweating profusely by the time we got to the fifth floor. We quickly stripped down to our tank tops and flopped on the bed to feast on our small pile of junk food. We didn't worry about getting crumbs on the bed covers because neither of us expected to be sleeping there. After quieting our hunger and thirst, we got back into our long pants and long-sleeved tops and masks and went back down to reception to exchange more cash, and then down to the street level and over to the market to pay our debt. At least our extra outing was absorbing some of the slow-ticking minutes on the clock.

The four-hour mark came and went. I paced in that tiny L-shaped space around the bed, shaking my arms out, practicing all sorts of breathing techniques, and trying to calm my central nervous system, which felt completely fried. Time crawled. Five hours. Six. It was 4:00 p.m. Our flight check-in time was 5:00 p.m. I felt panicked.

At 4:40 p.m., there was a knock on our door. It was Shifaau. He held up another sheet of paper with that same damn look on his face as Max had that morning. "It is positive," he announced. The room spun. I could not breathe. Wendy repeated, "It is positive." I sat down on the bed. Wendy stayed at the door talking to Shifaau. He told us that their government would require me to stay for fourteen days in quarantine. I immediately panicked, knowing that I could not stay here, in this room. My mental health would not survive. I needed a window. I needed to feel safe. I needed a desk to at least do some work, for crying out loud. I had a business to run on the other side of the world. I had two small dogs that were with a pet sitter who thought she would be going home tomorrow. I had so much I needed to figure out, and it all felt urgent. I heard Shifaau explaining that he had to be back on the boat at 5:00 p.m. for the next group of guests. He was leaving us in ten minutes. *Ten minutes!* Wait … what? What was I supposed to do? Wendy had the same time frame to get to the airport. I had ten minutes until I would lose everyone I knew and be utterly and completely alone in a foreign country literally on the other side of the planet from home, with COVID, without the proper clothing, and without very much cash. This was happening. This was real.

Shifaau's only suggestion to me was to book a hotel, not at a resort. A resort would likely take my temperature and ask me for proof that I did not have COVID, which I could not provide. They would not accept me. He told me to book a small hotel on Hulhumalé (an island extension of K.Malé, connected by a bridge) for all fourteen days, and counseled me that should they ask me about COVID I would need to lie. "They will not let you stay if they know you have COVID. We don't have any place for you to stay. They probably won't ask you, but if they do, you need to lie so you can stay."

I now had five minutes remaining. I speed-scrolled my way through Expedia and found the first small hotel that had thirteen nights' availability and also had a terrace so I could be outside during quarantine, as well as room service so I could eat without breaking my quarantine. These were my only search parameters. I whispered a prayer and paid a nonrefundable $2,000 USD, sight unseen, for what would be my home for the next two weeks.

From the other side of the tunnel I felt like I was in, I heard Wendy say, "I will stay with you, at least until you are okay." I was full-on crying again.

"I am not okay, Wendy. I am not going to be okay in five minutes or an hour or a day from now. You have to get on that plane. You cannot get stuck here with me. Here's the thing: I am going to cry. I can't help it. But you have to leave me anyway."

She nodded, tears in her eyes as well. This would be the hardest thing we had ever endured in our friendship, and we had walked beside one another for some really hard shit over the past fifteen years of our friendship, including divorces, parenting challenges, empty nesting, medical scares, and deaths of loved ones. Walking beside is very different from leaving someone behind. Wendy was the director of a school and could not be away longer than she already had been. If she stayed with me even just one night, she would have to take another PCR test because the rules at the time were that you had to fly within three days of testing, and we had been tested on Thursday. It was already Saturday. Even if she managed to get on a flight out the next day, the three-day period would expire before she got home. We had three legs to our flight and PCR tests would be checked at each departure, so she would not be allowed to board the flight on Sunday with a PCR test taken on Thursday since she would not arrive in the US until Monday, four days after the COVID test. If she had to retest, she would run the risk of testing positive, especially having been in such close proximity to me this whole time. That would mean she would then be quarantined there as well, and her fourteen days would start after mine had. Both of our inner little girls were being triggered by old wounds of abandonment and experiences of not feeling like we belonged—being left out, left behind, and just plain *left*. And yet we both still made the adult choice of the extremely painful but right thing to do. I was so proud of us for committing together to doing the hard thing and not making it mean that either of us chose the leaving, or that the act of separation said anything at all about who either of us was. And, while feeling proud and strong in this decision, I was also terrified. *I can do hard things*, I chanted in my head. It felt like a lie.

We left Shifaau sitting at the round table in the community space outside our rooms, speaking with the Russian couple about their options, and headed downstairs to the reception area where we were told we must pay our bill for the room. Inside, I felt a little offended that there was a charge for this holding cell, yet I did understand that this was obviously this man's place of business, and he would now have to deep clean and sanitize our room. After a few confusing attempts, we discerned that he wanted $65 USD, and cash only. This was unexpected. I had $80 USD and did not want to leave myself with only $15 for the next two weeks. Wendy had enough cash, so she paid him. He scrutinized every bill, one at a time. He held up a $20 bill and pointed to a microtear in the edge. "No good," he said.

"What do you mean?" we asked. He pointed to the ripped edge and looked at us like we should be ashamed of trying to pay with counterfeit money. Maybe there *should* be some shame around my country's general lack of regard or respect being so evident in the way we treat our paper currency–the tangible representation of our wealth and capitalism–predominantly crumpled, torn, and threadbare. We tried to explain to him that our money is always ripped and folded and bent. We promised him it was still good.

He probably did not understand most of what we were saying and just kept shaking his head no, pointing at the tear, thrusting the bill forward for us to see what he saw. Wendy dug out another $20 bill. Nope, that one also was not good. This almost put us over the edge. We were two girls in shock, on a very tight timeline, trying to get out of there, and from our perspective in that moment he was making it very challenging for us. Wendy leafed through her remaining cash and found two $10 bills that passed his exam. Okay then, one hurdle jumped. On to the next.

Shifaau joined us in the reception area and walked us down to the street level where he hailed us a taxi and put us in it before leaving us. Wendy was coming with me to the hotel so she could see where I would be. She needed at least that much. She also had some things she could transfer from her suitcase to mine that would help me, which had not occurred to us during all those hours of waiting in the room. I guess that shows how much we were both in denial of what was likely happening. Our taxi pulled up to the Planktons Beach hotel, and a young man helped me quickly check in. He carried both of our bags up another spiral staircase to the top floor. I thought to myself that it would be nice to be on the top floor. I did not expect to be doing those stairs very often, quarantined in my high tower, and the view would probably be better from up there.

The door at the top of the stairs opened onto a large terrace with Astroturf, which we walked across to a sliding glass door that the man unlocked and opened for us to enter. Wendy quickly popped open her suitcase on the bed. We each had only one pair of pants, so she left me hers so I would have something appropriate to wear if I was able to be outside at some point. She was traveling in a dress. She also had the power converter another friend, Jenny, had loaned us that we had not needed … until now. I had the plug adapter for charging my phone but would also need a converter to safely plug in my laptop. She gave me $50, which was all her remaining cash, withholding only the $5 she needed to get from the hotel to the airport. Mind you, $40 of that

$50 was those two "bad" $20 bills that the Tourist Inn would not accept. I had $80 of my own, so now potentially $130, but maybe only $90 if that $40 was truly unusable. It was also likely that some bills in my $80 would be unacceptable as well. Ninety dollars max, possibly less, to get through two weeks on my own. I had just paid my bill on the boat with $400 cash earlier that morning. Oh, what I would do to have that back now. Why didn't I use my credit card on the boat? I remember thinking that I was flying home and did not need a wad of cash in my backpack while traveling. Geez, I regretted that.

Suddenly, the very moment we had talked about less than an hour ago in that other hotel room was upon us. We both knew it. I cried, just as I knew I would. We hugged—a lingering, tight, clinging kind of hug. I had the conscious thought in that moment that I could die here, alone, and this could be my last hug ever.

My father had just died less than a year before of alpha-1 antitrypsin, a genetic disease that attacks the lungs. I am a carrier, meaning my body has less than the ideal amount of this protein to protect my lungs, so I had no idea what getting COVID might look like for me. Would it go to my lungs? Were my lungs my weak spot, like they had been for my father? Fear was barreling into the room dragging tunnel vision and darkness with it. All the unknowns swirled through my head like a tornado dropping debris in its path. Would I get sick? How sick? How would I get help if I needed it? What if I was unable to call or text someone to let them know I needed help? And who would that even be? Was I going to rely on my friends on the other side of the planet to somehow notify someone here that I needed help? Was the medical care on this island adequate? Was I going to survive this? Was I going to die alone in this room? Would it be days before anyone even discovered my body?

I did not walk back downstairs with Wendy. I did not wave to her from the terrace. I flopped facedown on my bed and cried my heart out.

It was 5:30 p.m. Longest. Day. Ever. I was understandably hungry, given that I had eaten only a few potato chips, a handful of nuts and raisins, and a couple of cookies. I ordered room service. While I waited for my food to arrive, I realized it was finally 6:30 a.m. at home. I could now update my family and friends, my assistants, and my pet sitter. I needed to call in the troops to support me from afar. My mobile carrier did not have international coverage in the Maldives, not even as an optional add-on, so I had turned my phone on airplane mode as I left the US to eliminate being charged expensive fees every time a random text came in. Knowing this, I had already made plans to use WhatsApp, a free international texting option, to stay in touch with my assistants and pet sitter during my vacation. I knew my sister already had WhatsApp on her phone when she had traveled with me to Morocco, where we had needed it for the same reason. So I used WhatsApp to text everyone the difficult news. My situation became very real as I had sad and scary conversations back-to-back with all those who needed to know. This is the compilation of the text conversation I had with my sister (also named Wendy) over the next forty-five minutes, while she relayed news to family members who did not yet have WhatsApp downloaded:

Me: I have some hard news. I have tested positive for COVID.

My sister: Honey!!! Oh, no! OMG, I'm so sorry. Where are you now? Hotel?

Me: Yes.

Sister: Are you symptomatic? Is everyone else on their way home?

*Me: No symptoms yet. Throat is a bit
sore, but I thought it was from the
testing swab. Now, I'm not sure.*

Sister: Are you safe in the hotel?

*Me: Yes. Wendy stayed with me until I got to a hotel.
She just left for the airport to try to get on our flight.
I am alone on the fucking other side of the planet.*

*Sister: You really are. This is going to take
all your courage. Did this all just happen?
How do you get food and meds?*

*Me: I got the news on the boat this morning.
Wendy opted to leave with me, which I am so
grateful for. I don't know how I will get food and
meds. I have room service available but no meds
or doctor. I had to leave the place where I got
tested. It didn't feel safe for me to be alone there.*

*Sister: That was so kind of Wendy. Is it
an English-speaking country?*

Me: No.

Sister: Is there Wi-Fi in the hotel?

*Me: Yes. They cannot know I tested positive or I
won't be allowed to stay. I can't be homeless here.*

Sister: I get it. So it's not like you test positive and they put you in a special hotel. You have to find a safe place to be. How long? Until a negative test? I want to scoop you up. I'm so, so sorry.

Me: 14 days.

Sister: Who has the dogs? What do you need from here, babe?

Me: My pet sitter can stay the nights but may need some help during the day on certain days.

Sister: I can go get them and bring them here. I know they're not used to other doggos, but that's an option.

Me: I think that might be more stressful for them. My pet sitter is good for all the nights I think.

Sister: Okay.

Me: I love you. Please, God, don't let me die alone over here ...

Sister: You're absolutely not going to die over there, my love. You are vaccinated and healthy. Do you know how to call their version of 911? What's the name and contact info of the hotel? Is there anyone you want me to get onto WhatsApp for you?

*Me: I know it's irrational … I'm just beyond
alone and potentially about to be very sick.*

*Sister: I'm here to talk 24/7. We will be
with you. Of course, you're afraid. I'm
with you. Is it evening for you now?*

Me: Yes. I am 11 hours ahead of you.

*Sister: Todd [our brother] is camping and
wanted you to know he'll be back to reliable
Wi-Fi tomorrow. He sends his love.*

Me: Thank you. Can you let my kids know please?

*Sister: Of course. I'll tell your kiddos. We're all
in a dither and full of thoughts and care for
you. We're far away and also very close.*

Me: Thank you.

*Sister: Talked with your kids. They are both getting
WhatsApp. Lois [my other best friend, who had
not been on the trip to the Maldives] is a hot,
sad mess on your behalf. You are SO loved.*

*Me: Thank you. Giant beetle in my room
and lizards everywhere … guess I'm going
to have to embrace island life. Fuck.*

*Sister: Oh god. Insult to injury. Can you send
pix of your room? How's the view?*

*Me: I have a magnificent balcony. It's
dark. I'll send pics tomorrow.*

I also heard from Max, the boat manager:

*Max: Max here from ScubaSpa. I got your
number from Julie [another girl in our group].
How are you doing out there? I received news
of the second test result. Have you received
information on what's to happen next for you?*

*Me: Hi, Max. I'm so relieved to hear from you.
Shifaau advised me to book a hotel for thirteen
nights and not mention that I tested positive,
so I have done that. I am at Planktons Beach
in Hulhumalé. Wendy is hopefully getting on a
plane right now, so I am alone. I don't know how
to change my flights or get retested or when ...
feeling pretty overwhelmed, honestly. This is scary.*

*Max: I can imagine that it is scary. I don't have much
experience (or any, rather) in such matters, but it
appears that the Health and Protection Agency
may want to put you into quarantine (which may
in fact take place at your current hotel, but I really
don't know). I'm going to get information from our
doctor regarding what options you might have. In the*

meantime, I would probably suggest that you contact any companies with which you have insurance coverage, and maybe feel around, or look over the policies, to see if this type of thing might be covered. You can contact me here if you have any questions or concerns with which I might be able to assist. It may be worthwhile to spend some time also trying to determine if any agencies in the US might assist somehow. I'm sorry that I don't have too much to offer you at the moment, but I'll try to gather up as much info as possible to help out. Until then, I imagine you realize that you should get some rest after such a hectic/emotional day. Everything will work out fine. Get some sleep tonight; put it out of your thoughts if you can, and I'll be in touch tomorrow with any updates. It's a very unfortunate situation, and I can imagine it must all be a bit overwhelming. Please do keep me posted on any progress! And ... well, as much as you can ... enjoy the extra vacation time.

I so badly wanted him to have a plan, to have resources for my care and safety. But that was not the case. He was back out at sea, and I was on my own. It was clear he cared about me as a human being and yet had no freaking clue how to help me or what options were even available to me. That last sentence of his, acting as though I were getting extra vacation time, was beyond adding insult to injury. That sentence would linger with me and taste bitter in my heart for days. He would not be the only person to say that to me. Others would naively comment that if I had to be stuck somewhere, at least I was on a beautiful tropical island. The intent behind these comments was meant to help me look on the bright side, but it was way too soon for a bright side and felt insensitive to the severity of my situation. Max did, however, provide me with the doctor's name and phone number for the clinic where I had been tested. Access to this doctor by phone would become my only sense of safety. So I forgave Max his lack of information or actual resources. He would continue to check in on me for the next few days, which was very kind. This pandemic thing was new to all of us. It should not have been a surprise that not everyone had a plan in place or that each country had different rules and processes. And yet, I *was* surprised. You don't realize you have assumptions in place until you come face-to-face with things being different than you apparently thought they would be.

The same guy who had carried my suitcase up to my room for me arrived carrying my plate of food. I would later learn that there were only two young men who worked here, Sahin and Rubel. They each worked twelve-hour shifts from either 8 a.m. to 8 p.m. or 8 p.m. to 8 a.m., seven days a week. They did everything, from running the reception desk, to room service deliveries, to maintenance, to housekeeping. Sahin shook his head no when I asked him to put the food on my room tab. He needed cash. I tried handing him my credit card. Nope. Cash. It took a bit for me to understand, but he patiently explained that the food was from a restaurant next door, and it needed cash payment. I had only $130 and felt unsafe spending any of it. He insisted, so I paid him cash. He, too, examined my $20 bill and rejected it. I tried the other one. No. Shit. So I truly did have only $90. I found acceptable bills and handed them over, now down another $10 in cash and knowing that room service was no longer an option. I would have to leave my room in the morning to find food and water that I could pay for with my credit card. The tap water was not safe for me to drink. I put the two unacceptable $20 bills in a separate compartment in my backpack. I looked at the remaining $80. I had quite a few more bills that would not pass; one was missing a corner, another had a significant rip, and a couple of others had similar small tears in the edges. I set those aside as well. I now had $38 in usable cash. Of that, I set three $5 bills aside. I knew I would need one of them to get to the clinic to retest at the end of my quarantine period, because that was what we had just paid our taxi to get from the clinic to the hotel, and then another $5 to get back to the hotel after the test. The taxi drivers there accepted only cash. I would need the final $5 to get to the airport to fly home at the end of this ordeal. That left me with $23 in cash that I could spend over the next two weeks unless I found a way to replenish my cash situation.

I sat on my bed to eat and looked around my room for the first time. There were swarms of tiny ants on the floor in several piles, one on each side of the bathroom door, with a trail of them running back and forth between the two swarms. Another swarm was on the floor next to the sliding glass door beside my nightstand. A large, black beetle scurried across the wall along the length of my headboard and disappeared behind the nightstand. I looked in the bathroom. It was another toilet-in-the-shower situation. No door for the shower. No toilet paper, just a hose sprayer attached to the wall like we have next to our kitchen sinks to rinse our dirty dishes at home. I assumed this was to be my new toilet paper experience. Tears trickled down my face yet again. I berated myself. I had to choose quickly, and I apparently chose badly. This was where I was stuck for the next fourteen days. I attempted to turn on the television, but … it would not turn on. It didn't work. The hits just kept coming. It was only 6:30 p.m. but it got dark at 6 p.m. there since we were so close to the equator, so I decided this day needed to be over. I climbed under the covers, one eye open for that damn beetle, and tried to sleep.

DAY TWO,
SEPTEMBER 26, 2021

I WOKE UP MY FIRST MORNING in this hotel room to an alarmingly loud storm outside, with rain pounding the roof and wind roaring. It felt like it might be unsafe out there. I wondered if it might be hurricane season on these islands. Even as I had the thought, I recognized that my mind was fear-mongering, and yet twenty-four hours ago worrying that my PCR test might come back positive would have seemed unnecessary and ridiculous as well. It seemed that no catastrophe was off the table.

It was dark when I checked in the previous night, so this was my first glimpse of my room in the light of day. The king-size bed took up much of the floor space and had four good pillows in white cases with matching white cotton sheets. There was no comforter, but there was no need for one with it being so hot. An air conditioning unit (that I had control over, thank goodness!) hung on the wall. On each side of the bed were very small side tables. I set my phone, a notebook to journal in, and a water bottle on the one closest to the door, which took up the entire surface area. The one on the other side of the bed had an old-school telephone, leaving no room for anything else, and the floor space was just wide enough to walk along the edge of the bed to get to the phone. Although, that was where the beetle had disappeared to the night before, so I would not be walking in that space *ever* during my stay. I decided if I needed the phone, I would crawl across the bed to reach it. Along the entire wall at the foot of the bed was a built-in desk, which did not include a chair, but I would ask for one so I could create a little workstation for myself and set up my laptop. I would consider that my office for the next two weeks. There were shelves underneath the desk on the right side, and on the top right of the desk was a small round tray with an electric pot to heat hot water for tea or instant coffee, two coffee cups, and a tiny teaspoon. On the far wall, just left of the desk, was an awkwardly placed window, only about a foot wide. A long, heavy curtain panel covered it, and I saw no reason to pull the curtain back because the view was of an apartment building across a very narrow alley. There were rows of balconies on the other building, with clotheslines on each. We probably could have passed a cup of tea back and forth from our windows if I didn't have the equivalent of the plague. I left the curtain closed. A large mirror hung above the desk (so I guess I would be able to watch myself work), but there was no artwork on any of the walls. The view through my sliding glass door of the ocean in the distance was what salvaged the room from being quite utilitarian and dismal. At the foot of my bed, just to the right of the desk, was the door to the bathroom, which included a sink, a western toilet with a spray hose (not a bidet) hanging on the wall, and a shower with no door or separation from the toilet. I had one bath-size towel, no washcloths or hand towels, and—worth mentioning again—no toilet paper. The bath towel was stiff and scratchy, probably from having been line-dried, and was thin and well-worn with frayed edges. At home, this would now be relegated to the rag bin. There, it was the guest towel. In theory, there would be just enough room to put a yoga mat on the floor between the bed and the sliding glass door. I would, however, never lie on this floor, yoga mat or not. The flooring was white tile and made it easy to see swarms of tiny ants. They definitely bite. I already had evidence of that on my feet, ankles, and shins.

The stairs from the lobby led to the terrace. What I did not realize the night before was that there were two rooms that shared the terrace. My room was the closest to the stairs, and there was another one on the far side of the terrace, sharing the wall my bed was against. So my terrace was communal, which translated to *unusable* during my quarantine when there were guests in the other room.

I became symptomatic, which was oddly validating and also scary as hell. I took a few minutes to assess my physical situation. I had a ridiculously painful headache, and I wondered if it was from the stress, from being hungry and dehydrated, or a symptom of COVID. The answer was probably just yes. It was from all of it. My nose was stuffy, I felt pressure inside my ears, and my throat was sore. I touched my own forehead and decided that I probably did not have a fever yet, but it was hard to tell. It was hot here, so of course I felt hot. I didn't have a thermometer to check. I did, however, pack a bag of vitamin C lozenges. I was thinking it wouldn't hurt to boost my immunity while I traveled. I counted those out and divided by fourteen, the number of days I would be in quarantine. I had enough for four or five lozenges per day. I made a few piles of five and promised myself I would make sure I went through one pile each day. I also had some ibuprofen. It was not much, so I would need to use it sparingly until I could get more. And … oh my gosh … I suddenly remembered that the me who had been packing my bag a lifetime ago had tossed in a box of Mucinex at the last minute. One of my travel companions had mentioned she was bringing some just in case, because it might be hard to get things like that if we should need them, and we were traveling in a COVID world now. Wow! Providential. I sent gratitude to Laura and whichever angels nudged her to share that valuable information with me. I retrieved them from a deep pocket in my backpack and counted them out as well. The recommended dose was two capsules every four-to-six hours. I definitely did not have enough for that. I would need to take one at a time and string them out as long as I could in between. But it was something. I was grateful.

This was all very overwhelming. Not only was I now symptomatic, but I also felt emotionally flooded and completely isolated. I had only the leftover snacks from what Wendy and I purchased the day before at that little market and one partial bottle of water. I swallowed my first Mucinex capsule with a couple of swigs of the water and thought to myself that I could not afford to get dehydrated because that could make me sicker. I realized I might have to go out in this storm for food and water. Everything felt so hard. My nervous system was fried from the past twenty-four hours.

I had a growing mental list of things I needed to take care of administratively. Life at home would go on with or without me. I needed to engage the best I could from here and hand off or cancel anything I couldn't take care of remotely. I got paid with physical checks mailed to me, so I would need someone to go through my mail, pull out the checks, use my business stamp to endorse them, and take them to the bank to deposit for me to keep my cash flow working to pay bills that would come due while I was quarantined. Fortunately, most of my bills were already set up on auto-draft and the others could all be paid electronically. I messaged my friend Lois to ask if she could perhaps do this for me a few times over the next two weeks. Her home was close enough to mine to ask this favor of her.

"Of course, love bug!" she exclaimed. She calls everyone "love bug." It is so endearing and was especially so at this moment. She also told me she was in touch with Robin, my pet sitter, and would go over a few times to be with my dogs while the pet sitter had other things she needed to do that would take longer than I normally left them alone. I felt a rush of love for these women who loved my fur babies as if they were me in my absence. I then messaged Robin and asked her to send me photos of my weekly planner pages for the next two weeks since she was staying in my home. I had no idea if I had appointments that I would need to reschedule. It turned out that I did. Of course I did. I started a written list of things I would need to do. Not today, though. Today, it would be all I could do to get food and water. First things first. My wellness was the *only* priority at the moment. This was new. My self-care had always been the thing that I could postpone without guilt, because getting everything else done was more important, or at least more visible. The irony was palpable.

The storm subsided. I grabbed the opportunity and threw on the same clothes I wore all day the day before since they were the only items of clothing that were appropriate for me to wear in public. I was saving Wendy's pants for the flight home since mine would be filthy by then. I stepped out onto the terrace to look around outside. The heat and humidity wrapped themselves around me like a sticky hug. My bare feet squished in the wet AstroTurf. There was a round patio table with four chairs and an umbrella for dining al fresco. There were two low stadium chairs ideal for sitting in the sun to read. On the right, was a raised plunge pool that looked pretty with blue tile work. It had no water in it, but rather, several little resident lizards. I walked to the far edge of the terrace and looked down on a narrow cobblestone street. Quite a few mopeds were parked on the far edge as these were how the people who worked at this hotel and the surrounding restaurants and markets along this stretch of beach commuted to work. Directly on the other side of the street was the beach. One step up a curb and I would be immediately standing on the sand. There were a few bushes growing in the sand and a row of very tall breezy trees. They reminded me of some type of willow, but I had no idea what kind of trees they were. I tried to look them up at some point, but none of the trees found in the Maldives that came up in my Google search looked like them. They were light and airy and majestic, and through them I could see the sea just beyond. A couple of picnic tables stood under their shade, near the street. I held my hands to my heart to encourage myself. The view from there would help me get through the isolation of my quarantine. Something was okay.

I slipped on my one pair of shoes that covered my feet, and double masks since I knew I was contagious, and descended the stairs to the lobby where Sahin was still on shift. We had a little bit of a language barrier, but his English was generally pretty good once I could find the words he understood.

"Buy food?" … He thought I wanted room service again.

"No. Shop for food?" … He thought I wanted to exchange some of my money for their currency.

"No. Market?" … Yes! There it is!

"What time does it open?" He shook his head signaling he didn't understand.

"Can I go now?" He motioned for me to follow him, and this sweet young man walked with me a block and a half to the little market. I was so grateful to him for this act of kindness, and grateful that the market was so close.

The men inside did not speak English. I showed one of them my credit card with a questioning look and asked, "Okay?" He nodded and pointed to the credit card machine next to him by the register. One of the men then followed me around the store, right next to me. I mean, all up in my business. If he had not had a mask on, I would have felt his breath on me. Even though we had a total of three masks between us, I still felt concerned for him. I wondered if this was their general practice to have one of them follow each shopper, or was it because I was a tourist, or did he maybe not trust me, or did he think I might need help? Regardless, it was awkward! I did not know what I wanted, and I did not even know what a lot of the things on the shelves were. Labels were not in English, and packaging was not familiar. The storefront was quite small, and the aisles were narrow. I literally walked each aisle slowly about three times through, sticking my face right up to items to try to figure out what they were. There was a tiny produce section about the width of my arm span with several things I did not recognize. I was willing to try something new, but there were just two or three of each thing, and they all looked like they would require things I did not have access to, like a knife to peel them or a stove to cook them. There were a few giant carrots. I mean, *giant*. Each carrot was the size of an English cucumber. I selected one of those, thinking I could nibble on it for a few days. I found peanut butter and a half-loaf of sliced bread. (It was so interesting to see that they separated the loaves into two bags.) Cans of tuna that had pop-tops would be good protein for me, and they had lots of flavors. I had noticed on the boat that Maldivians eat a lot of tuna. Okay … when in Rome, right? I selected four different flavors and added them to my basket. I found a little bag of muesli and a box of coconut milk–score! I knew I had a coffee mug and a tiny spoon meant to stir my tea in the room, so I could eat cereal from the mug with the baby spoon. I was feeling very resourceful now.

I turned to my shopping assistant and asked, "Medicine for headache?" I pointed to my head and made what I thought was a face expressing pain, and then realized I had a mask on so I was certain it was lost on him. "Ouch. Pain," I said, motioning again to my head. He shook his head no. He said a word that sounded like "pharmacia" and pointed outside. Crap. I did not have the bandwidth to find a pharmacy and try to get what I needed. I let it go. I would make do with the ibuprofen, rationed Mucinex, and vitamin C lozenges.

I turned back to this man and asked, "Water?" Yes. Oh, thank God. He led the way to a tiny cooler with several larger 1,500-mL bottles of water lined up on the bottom shelf. He held up one finger with a questioning look on his face. I shook my head and did a quick calculation of how many I thought I could carry back to the hotel and up all those stairs to my room. Water bottles would be heavy, and I could already tell they would take every ounce of strength I had, yet water was essential to my survival. I held up four fingers. He nodded, grabbed them for me, and carried them to the cash register. I followed him. I had found everything I thought I could eat that would not require a can opener, or utensils I didn't have access to, or need some manner of cooking.

I had no microwave or fridge in my room. Part of me wanted to cry when I looked at my groceries. This sad little pile of food would need to sustain me for however long I might be sick. I had no idea how sick I might get, or when I would be able to walk back over to the market. I knew I could not carry any more than I had on the counter, and I had no cash to tip the young man to help me carry more. It would have to do. I handed my credit card to the man behind the register when he showed me my total of 229.70 Rufiyaa. I had no idea how much that was in US dollars, and honestly, I didn't care. It was worth it, whatever it was. (It turned out it was only about $18 USD!)

My shopping assistant put the items in bags for me, and I carried them back to the hotel, quietly taking in the sights on the street as I walked. It was mostly construction zones along the sidewalks, and there was that narrow alley off to my right with laundry strung on ropes outside the windows that I could see from the tiny window by my desk. I walked inside the hotel and stopped briefly at the front desk to request a chair for the desk in my room. I then began my ascent up those spiral stairs. I required several stops along the way to catch my breath. I was sweating profusely and surprisingly dizzy. I made it to my room, unpacked my bags onto a shelf under the desk, which I decided would now be my pantry, and flopped onto my bed to rest for a few minutes.

Next on my agenda was to set up my laptop and check on my business. Back home in my real life, I run a real estate transaction management company, with two part-time assistants who I left in charge of my business for the ten days I was to be on vacation. As an entrepreneur, this was the first time in five years that I had anyone to support my clients while I took a vacation, so I had truly unplugged and leaned into taking real time off. I had not brought my other cell phone, the one designated strictly for business. It helped me maintain better boundaries by having a separate phone. So I had left that phone at home and had decided to bring my laptop only at the last minute "just in case" I had a delay or something big needed my attention.

Before I left home, I had set up a WhatsApp channel for my assistants and me and named our group chat "The Bat Signal." When I created it, I was thinking it would be the way they could signal me if they really needed my help with something. This felt ironic now, and also serendipitous. It turned out that I was the one who had to send the Bat Signal out to them: "Guess what? You are going to be doing this a couple more weeks." They were in over their heads and handling it like champions. The training I had given them had been meant to just provide a little extra support to my clients for the eight business days I was to be on vacation, not to fully do my job. But with the added two weeks for my quarantine, it was the equivalent of showing someone a video about how to swim and then throwing them in the deep end of the pool to apply what they had just learned. I was grateful that the workaholic in me had won the internal battle to pack my laptop so I could tap back in and work as I felt able. Although the time difference would create some challenges for sure, it would help me pass time in the room and keep me from worrying that my business might suffer in my prolonged absence. I did not need anything else to worry about. There was enough of that already.

I set up the converter and selected the correct plug adapter and hesitantly hit the power button, hoping that I set it all up correctly and this wouldn't kill my laptop. Whew! It worked! I was officially connected to the world! The *elation* of that moment ... you just have no idea. I went through my transactions and my emails and was relieved to see that my assistants had done a fabulous job. My emails were current, and they had left excellent notes for me about what was happening or what was outside their scope and needed my attention. The confirmation that exactly the right people were working for me caused another surge of gratitude. I threw my arms in the air above my head, tilted my face back, and spoke it out loud over and over: "THANK YOU, THANK YOU, THANK YOU."

Dr. Usama, the doctor from the clinic in Malé, messaged me on WhatsApp. He had contacted the boat for my information. When I responded to his text, he called me through the app. His English was superb, and I felt so relieved to be in contact with a doctor. Apparently, he had wanted me to stay at the Tourist Inn from the day before because it was near enough to his clinic that he could pop in and check on me to monitor my symptoms and provide medical care if needed. No one had explained that to me or Shifaau. I was actually glad I did not know because I am such a rule-follower that I would have stayed there, and that would have been awfulness on top of awfulness. He understood that I had not known I was meant to stay there and was very compassionate. However, the doctor informed me that the HPA (the Maldivian Health Protection Agency) was looking for me. Staff from the HPA had been calling him at least once, and sometimes twice, every hour wanting to know where I was. This was extremely alarming news! He said they wanted to know that I was actually quarantined, since I did not stay at the Tourist Inn. I told the doctor that I was not hiding from anyone, and he could absolutely tell them the name of my hotel and share my WhatsApp number with them. I assured him that I was self-quarantining, and that I had booked and prepaid my room for the full fourteen days required by the government. He said he would pass along that information to the HPA, and then told me that he could travel to my hotel tomorrow if I would like for him to visit me. We agreed that I would WhatsApp him by noon tomorrow to update him on how I felt and decide then if I wanted him to come. He assured me that he would help get me any medicine I needed if my symptoms became more severe. Just knowing this made me feel so much better. At least I knew who I could call if I needed medical assistance. Perhaps I would not die in this room after all.

But now I had a new fear to add to the pile. I was *wanted* by the Maldivian government! I felt like a criminal they were actively tracking down. I started imagining men in hazmat suits from the HPA showing up to escort me back to the Tourist Inn for my quarantine. My room had a lot of issues, but it was considerably better than that holding cell I was in the day before. *Please let me just stay here.* Irony, huh? This room that I had not felt safe in now felt like my safe place.

Months later, after my return home, I saw news stories about people being arrested in other countries for "fleeing" their quarantine hotel and being charged with jeopardizing public safety. It had not occurred to me that I could be arrested. I imagined being taken to a worse hotel room, not a jail cell! While I support global health safety, I experienced firsthand that there were not always protocols in place in other countries to help visitors know how and where to stay put, and there were language barriers to communicate that as well. I cannot imagine getting arrested for trying to solve my own problem of basic human needs for shelter, food, and water in the middle of the stress of being sick with COVID-19 and quarantined in a foreign country. In hindsight, I am grateful I was naive to that possibility.

Because the doctor had just called me through WhatsApp, I now realized I could use it to call home. I did not know WhatsApp could be used for anything other than texts. This was wonderful news! I called my sister and then my mom. We cried and talked, and we all felt a little better just to hear each other's voices. They both asked how they could get money to me. I couldn't make it to an ATM. I had already checked. The nearest one would be a twenty-minute walk. I was already too weak to manage that walk, and even if I could, I should not leave my room again while I was symptomatic. They both admitted they were scared for me because no one except the doctor knew I was sick, and they were worried about how I would get food and water. *I know. Me too.*

The sliding door to my room off the shared terrace apparently opened from both sides. I had not noticed that. So far, I had come and gone the way I entered with Sahin when he carried my bags up the previous night. I locked the door on the right side where the handle was, the way that sliding doors normally worked. And suddenly, a few minutes later, a random man slid my door open from the left side and just stepped through the long curtains into my room. I froze in fear. He did not say a word and quickly backed out upon seeing me sitting there on my bed, so he clearly did not intend me any harm. I don't think he spoke English, and judging from his facial expression, he was just as startled as I was. My guess is that he had just checked into the other room off our shared terrace and had gotten confused about which sliding door was his. After he left, I examined that side of the door, and while there was not a handle on that side, you could place your hands on the metal frame or flat on the glass and slide it open. There was a deadbolt in the floor from the inside that locked it in place, but that clearly did not work. It looked like it was locked, but the door could still slide open. I pulled the deadbolt open and then back in–it was fully engaged–but still the door easily slid open. It was as if Fear had a full-access backstage pass to my life. Nothing was off limits, and I had just discovered that the panic room meant to be my safe space in a crisis had no freaking lock. *Hello vulnerability. Is there any other semblance of my sense of safety remaining that we can strip away? Oh God, I hope not.*

I opened the peanut butter and used my finger to smear some onto a slice of bread. I bit into it and … nothing. I tasted nothing. Well, that was honestly probably a gift at that point. I mean, look at my food options—lol! I ate the bread. I noticed how it felt in my mouth. There was comfort in the sticky chewiness of it.

The other guy who worked there, Rubel, knocked on my door. I opened the curtain to see him standing there smiling, holding a chair for my desk. It was my first time meeting him. He wondered if I needed anything–room service or anything else. I asked him about my television not working. He requested permission to step inside, so I said yes and grabbed my mask and put it on as he stepped inside. I struggled with some guilt about allowing him inside my contagious COVID den. Wanting my television to work won out over the integrity of avoiding potentially exposing him. I am not proud of that moment. It was just reality. I stayed back from him as far as I could in my little room while he fiddled with cords and buttons for a few minutes and then, voila! It worked. I had TV! I clapped my hands in delight. Next, I pointed to the anthills on either side of the bathroom door. He said he would take care of it. Then I showed him that my door would not lock. He laughed and said, "No one coming in."

"Someone already did!" I exclaimed. "A man walked right in!" I am not sure if he understood, but he said he would tell someone. I felt self-conscious and did not want to be seen as the high-maintenance American princess that I recognized I probably looked like to him at that point (and honestly, I know I can be a little high-maintenance, especially when I travel, but wanting a television that works, a door that locks, and no bugs in my room did not seem too extra to me). I swallowed hard and asked for one more thing—a hand towel or washcloth. He didn't know what I meant, so I pointed to my one bath towel and made hand gestures to show I wanted "smaller" and held up two fingers. He nodded. A little while later, he came back with two hand towels. I designated one to dry myself after using the hose to rinse whenever I used the toilet. I set that one on the back of the toilet so it would not get confused with the other one, which I planned to use on my bed as a placemat/plate to eat on. I had saved the lid from the Pringles can from yesterday's snack run and had been using that as a little tray for portions of the leftover trail mix. *I will make this work. I am so resourceful!*

I texted via WhatsApp with a friend who asked if there was anything she could do to help. "I don't want you to feel like you are left alone over there," she wrote.

I thought to myself, *Well, I am.* I knew how much support I had on the other side of the world, but as well-intentioned as they were, they could not be *in it* with me. Even when our support systems can be physically present with us, we are ultimately alone in the darkness of crisis. They can hug us, hold our hand, pray for us, whisper encouragement in our ears, bring flowers and meals, and just sit beside our beds. Yet, at the end of the day, they have their own lives to return to. I have been on both sides of this. It feels bad to leave someone who is hurting, and yet we cannot give up our responsibility to our own lives to be fully present constantly, and even with all the time and love we can give, we know they are still inside of it in a place where we cannot join them. It is as if crisis is an impenetrable, dark bubble. The person in crisis is inside, alone. Even in a shared crisis like the loss of a family member, those affected are inside their own bubble, processing and grieving in their own way. Those outside are loving observers, tending to basic needs. The crisis is not theirs to own, and they could not step inside even if they wanted to. For me, on the other side of the world, this crisis bubble felt like it was suspended by a rope over the edge of a cliff. I was out of reach, and my loved ones could not even directly observe or do much to tend to my basic needs. Because of our time difference, when they were awake worrying and wondering about me, I was asleep. I imagined it was an incredibly helpless feeling. And on my end of the rope, the fibers were brittle and losing strength, leaving me dangling by a few untrustworthy threads and looking up at Fear, holding a pair of scissors.

DAY THREE,
SEPTEMBER 27, 2021

AT LEAST, I thought it was day three. It felt like it could be day forty-seven. I had mostly slept and watched movies in bed for the past twenty-four hours, and time had slipped into irrelevance.

Everyone who had been there with me on vacation had now arrived home. They were all chatting on our group text thread in WhatsApp about getting their bodies back to the US time zone and testing for COVID (in case they got it from me or other travelers on their way home). They were sharing stories of getting back to their regular lives. From this end, it felt shitty to see their texts to each other. While the days and specific time on the clock in my here and now felt inconsequential to my life in this room, as I watched those text exchanges among my friends I was measuring time by where I felt I "should" be, had things gone according to plan. The awareness of this reminded me that I was not in the present moment. I was somewhere else, in an imagined future, and that could not be helpful to my overall wellness.

I woke up to the sound of the call to prayer at 4:40 a.m. I guess I could not hear it the day before because of the storm. I fell in love with the call to prayer on a trip to Morocco a couple of years before. There was something about the community of it, and the vibration of the sung prayers over the poor-quality speakers, sharing the same scratchy-popping aesthetic as the older vinyl records I love listening to. I lay in the darkness and let it wash over me like a soothing balm to my soul and drifted back to sleep.

I woke up about an hour later. When my eyes fluttered open I was facing my sliding door, and I could see the most spectacular sunrise through the trees over the sea. I shuffled out onto my terrace to watch, in awe of the hope and renewal it filled me with. I glanced to the left and realized with delight that the mosque was right next door. I could see the tower with the speakers. Upon arrival on this island before boarding our boat, I had asked about the call to prayer because I longed to hear it again. I had been told then that there was only one mosque on the island, and it was north of where we were. Here it was—the only mosque in Hulhumalé! In this moment, I knew I was in exactly the right place. Choosing this hotel was not haphazard, although it felt that way in those terrifying moments. I did not know what I was doing as I made my selection, but I was clearly being guided. Even with all the things I labeled as "bad" about it in my first twenty-four hours, I now saw why I was there, in this specific hotel. I would be gifted with the call to prayer five times a day the entire time I was there, and with fourteen glorious sunrises to wake up to. I was right across the street from the beach. I could see the ocean from my terrace. Yes, I had COVID. And yet, life was good. I was Sourced. Everything my soul needed was being provided for me by my higher power. My mind and body did not feel safe, and yet the Universe was showing me that I was being watched over and resourced and loved on. Now, if I could just find a way to lean into that with trust that my whole experience and wellness on the physical and mental realms were also already covered.

DAY THREE, SEPTEMBER 27, 2021

I found myself talking out loud to myself a lot that day. I do this a lot at home as well, because I live alone. But even I realized this behavior was extra. I wondered, ironically also aloud, if I perhaps needed a "Wilson" to talk to, like Tom Hanks did in *Cast Away*. I did feel a bit cast away, and a little like I was surviving alone on a deserted island. I know, that's a bit extreme. But it made me giggle, and in that moment, it signaled that my sense of humor was returning. This was such a good sign to me.

The loop playing in my head was that I got left here. Somewhere inside me this had triggered abandonment fears. But this was not the truth. I had not been abandoned. I needed to reframe my mindset. There were still some dark places in my head trying to creep out into the daylight. I was not at all certain I was going to survive this. I texted my daughter to remind her, in the event I got worse, that she had financial power of attorney for me and that my sister had medical power of attorney. She ignored my comments and offered to wire funds to me to help with my cash situation. So I filled her in on the information I gave my mom and sister the day before—that the closest place I could have money sent would be a twenty-minute walk from where I was. I was not strong enough for that, nor should I be exposing all the people along the way and inside that bank. Then she told me she would fly out there if I needed her to. I loved her extra in that moment. I wanted her to come, to be there with me, in this with me—someone to stroke my hair and feel my forehead and make sure I had water and food and medicine. And, I knew it was not practical or necessary. I was not dying. I did not need to be in hospital. Although my internal darkness added a quiet "yet" to both of those statements, I knew that having someone fly halfway around the world to expose themselves to COVID in my tiny room with me would be irresponsible. But just knowing that she would come if things got worse and I needed her, that I would not die there alone—that was everything.

I also heard from my son via WhatsApp. He worked crazy restaurant hours (even worse during the pandemic), so this was his first day off since he got the news about my quarantine. It was good to hear from him. He sent me love and healing vibes and asked if there was anything he could do for me. I told him to just keep checking in. Knowing he was thinking about me would be helpful for my mindset. My rational mind knew that it was the time difference that kept my phone silent all day long, and yet my story of abandonment fed on that silence as proof that I was not cared about or loved. *Out of sight, out of mind,* chanted my insecurities.

I went back to bed. I spent most of the day there. I was sleeping a lot. Days and nights were interchangeable. I was grateful for the blackout curtains in my room and was just going with it. I felt achy and exhausted in a way I never had before. It was as though I were swimming through mud, exerting muscles to just roll over, let alone walk the few steps to the bathroom. I nibbled on a few bites of food every time I woke up and drank a little water and sucked on the occasional vitamin C lozenge. I tasted nothing. I did feel a little better than I had the previous afternoon and night. I had developed a tickly cough that was happening more often, but it was not painful or persistent and did not feel like it was affecting my breathing at all. I still ached all over. My head hurt especially bad, my nose was stuffy and drippy, and I was super dizzy. However, I still did not have a fever.

So I sent Dr. Usama a WhatsApp text to cancel the appointment we had arranged for that day. While I felt pretty awful, I rationalized that it wasn't bad enough to warrant him traveling all the way across the island to see me. To be completely honest, I was worried that his visit might blow my cover. Would Rubel or Sahin realize he was a doctor visiting me? Would he say something to them on his way in or out that would alert them to my condition? What would happen to me if they knew? Would I be moved to that room without windows, far away from the beach? I did not want to risk that unless my symptoms felt scarier than the prospect of being removed from there. I told Dr. Usama that it was comforting to me to know I had an appointment with him if I needed it and asked if we could do that again for the next day. He called me and explained that he had no time available the next day but he could come the evening after that if needed. We set that up tentatively, and I was to check in with him again that morning to confirm or cancel.

I asked the doctor where the Russian couple was staying. I wondered if they had remained at the Tourist Inn or had also gone rogue like me. Shockingly, they had managed to fly home within hours of my departure from them on that first day. The doctor explained to me that Russia did not require a negative PCR test to enter the country, so they had found a direct flight from the Maldives to Russia on an airline that did not require a negative PCR test to board since the destination country did not require it. What? I felt judgmental of them for flying home knowing she was COVID-positive, exposing everyone on that flight. It certainly was a selfish choice they had made. And yet, I admit I also felt impressed (and honestly, jealous) that they had found a way to circumvent a two-week quarantine on this island. The doctor lamented that there were not any direct flights to the US from the Maldives for me to have had the same option, but that would not have mattered as the US was requiring negative COVID tests to enter. So I was truly the only one left there in quarantine.

Using the toilet was frustrating, and also … hilarious. I could not seem to master getting the angle of the sprayer right. It was quite forceful. There was no control of the volume of water, just on or off. If I aimed from the front, the water spray was angled too far down and caused a tsunami of toilet water on my butt, and if I aimed from behind it was always angled a bit too far up and the overspray shot out between my legs and onto the toilet seat and even the tile wall in front of me. Either way, I got myself wet, along with parts of the bathroom. I had been struggling with which towel to use—the one I would dry off with after a shower (when I eventually had the energy to shower) and would prefer to be clean against my skin, or the one I had designated for use under my food, which obviously didn't feel like a sanitary choice, or the one I had wiped my nether-regions with post-rinse? That's the one that won by default. I didn't have the energy to deal with figuring out how to dry my wet clothes either. At some point, it did occur to me that I could just get naked before I went in the bathroom each time, so that helped with the wet clothing. And then I appreciated the convenience of the toilet being in the shower. At least I didn't have to wipe down the walls or the floor from the overspray.

I had the energy to stand a little longer, so I took advantage of already being naked and in the shower and turned on the actual shower for the first time. There was a little trial-size bottle of watery shower gel next to the sink but no shampoo or conditioner. I did not bring any with me since the yacht had luxury bath products in the bathrooms. So I just used the water to rinse my hair of several days' worth of sweat. It was still an improvement.

Sahin came up in the afternoon with an aerosol can of bug spray. He sprayed all the visible bugs and their trails. It probably smelled awful and toxic, but I could not smell it—another little gift inside the illness. I was just glad most of the bugs were dead now. I noticed a few survivors after Sahin left, but I just shrugged those off. Maybe the remnants of the spray would take care of them with time. It was feeling really gross in the room. Everywhere I looked there were bugs. It surprised me how quickly I was able to just accept that we were roommates. I had a ton of bug bites all over me, especially on my legs. They were terribly itchy, made even more so due to the heat, and my legs were a bit swollen. Hopefully, those could begin to heal.

DAY FOUR,
SEPTEMBER 28, 2021

I WOKE UP WITH A HEAVY BLANKET of sadness over me. I could not stop crying. The weight of what was happening to me was wearing me down. I had lived alone for the past seven years and actually thought I enjoyed being alone—something I had learned to do after my divorce. It took years to tune into my own company and to build a life I truly enjoyed living on my own. I had achieved that and really found fulfillment in my alone time, even working from home now. But *this* type of alone … it was more alone than alone ever aloned. It was a whole new level of alone. My tribe was literally on the other side of the planet. Our time zones did not sync up. I could not choose to be alone or not be alone. I was just *alone*. A Lone. Lonely. Deeply lonely.

And … the Universe responded. My friend Liezel, who had been on the vacation with me, texted me via WhatsApp and asked permission to share my situation with a group we were both a part of called AWE (Academy of Women Emerging), a group for female entrepreneurs that I had been involved in for three years. I had my personal tribe of close friends, and I also had this tribe. It was not just about our businesses. As your life was, so your business was, and vice versa. Our fears and growth edges showed up in both and reflected back to us in all areas of life. These women and coaches knew me intimately. It had not occurred to me that they did not yet know about my situation because two of the eleven friends I took this vacation with were from my AWE group. And yet, in hindsight, of course they did not share my experience with the group without my permission. These were women of high integrity who understood what was theirs to share and what was not. I gave my permission with a sigh of relief, realizing that more connection was on the way. One by one, the AWE women found their way onto WhatsApp and talked to me. This became another lifeline for me.

One of them asked me how I was feeling. My response: "Lightheaded, sad, bored, stuffy, achy, tired, trapped, frustrated, grateful, loved … it's quite the spectrum!"

My assistants had been notifying my clients, and they were also starting to check in on me as the word spread. Some of our conversations went like this:

Client: Hi Janine, just heard your unfortunate news. Wanted you to know I'm thinking about you and sending you all the positive vibes and prayers. Let me know if you need anything.

Me: Thank you. I'm ok. This is hard in all the ways. I'll make it through, one day at a time.

Client: I can't even imagine. Is there anyone else in quarantine with you? Are you staying somewhere comfortable? We're with you in spirit.

*Me: I am completely alone. No one to even
resource me, so I have to get my own food
and water every couple of days. No kitchen
access, just bed and bathroom, so eating tuna
from can and peanut butter from jar.*

*Client: Oh Janine. I'm so sorry. Sending you all the
prayers and positivity. I know you'll find a way to see
the positive in this somehow, however hard it is now.
I'm sure you're going to learn so much about yourself.*

How true that was.

I did log in and do some work that morning, which was Monday late afternoon at home. I knew my emails would not be responded to until their Tuesday morning, which would be that night for me, but at least I could make myself useful and plug back into my life at home for little bits at a time. I tired quickly, sitting at my computer and focusing on so many contractual details, but it felt good to do something normal.

Fun new development: I was lying on my bed and … I literally just shit myself. No warning. Didn't even think I had a gas bubble. Just … bloop … and out it oozed into my shorts. That was not a fun experience to clean up with my lack of towels or soap. I will spare you any further details. But now I was concerned that something I'd been eating might not be good. I could not taste anything, so I could not know if something went bad unless it was visually off. I looked it up and learned that diarrhea can also be a symptom of COVID-19. I did not know which it was. It made me feel a little gaggy, thinking that I may have eaten something that went bad and not even known it. If it was something I ate that caused the diarrhea, I needed to stop eating it. I weighed throwing away what little food I had left that might still be good, leaving myself unable to eat much until I could get back to the store, against continuing to eat what was potentially making me sicker. This was a difficult decision because I had no way to know either way, but I would be stuck with pretty severe consequences if I made the wrong choice.

I had also been extremely dizzy that day. It was definitely worse. I needed water and more food, but knew I could not successfully make it to the market and back. I could barely walk to the bathroom without supporting myself on the bed, then the doorframe, and then the bathroom walls, each step of the way. I was concerned about becoming dehydrated since I was nearly out of water and now had diarrhea.

I made the difficult decision to splurge on room service. It was scary to use any more of my cash, but it was even scarier in that moment to think I could potentially get sicker due to poor nutrition and lack of water. I carefully added up my options so I would stay within my available $23 cash. I realized this would likely be my last actual meal until I got home, but I decided I needed to be okay with spending everything I had to get myself healthy, because once I was healthier I would be able to walk to the market to buy more food and water with my credit card. If I got more depleted than I was now, I would not be able to get what I would need. I bravely ordered rice with chicken and a fresh fruit plate and three big bottles of water, for a total of $21. The rice arrived in a shaped upright cylinder with a fried egg on top, which delighted me—more protein than I expected, *and* it was pretty. I could not taste it, and yet it was wonderful! The texture and the warmth of the rice were comforting. I recognized and was grateful for the nourishment this food was providing me, and it also just felt so good to no longer feel hungry after eating. I had been eating to sustain; it warded off feeling uncomfortably hungry but never provided that satisfied feeling. This was different. I had more than I could consume available to me, something I was used to and took for granted at home. I silently acknowledged the ways in which I had been unaware of many of my privileges. I saved the fruit plate for later. It was large enough to be several meals for me the next day.

The people in the room next door had checked out, so the terrace was all mine again. It was rainy, but hopefully soon I would be able to sit out there for a bit of sun and vitamin D between rainstorms.

DAY FIVE,
SEPTEMBER 29, 2021

IN THE MIDDLE OF THE NIGHT, I went to the bathroom and realized I was getting used to hosing off my va-jay-jay. I was able to do everything in the dark and go right back to sleep after, even though I had just sprayed myself with very cold water. Progress!

I slept well again but woke to another heavy, sad morning. I missed greeting my days with happiness and enthusiasm. I've always been a morning person and usually woke up with energy and positivity. But in that room, each day just felt like a long, sprawling thing to get through. Questions about what I was going to do today made me feel cranky, even when I was the one asking.

Physically, I felt noticeably better. The food and water from last night definitely helped. I did still have symptoms, but less so. My head felt sort of dazed ... sleep foggy ... it was hard to put words to it, but it was like I was under water, everything was in slow motion, and I was an observer of my own life. Maybe this was COVID brain or COVID fog? I was also coming out of what had likely been a state of shock. The last few days had been pretty traumatizing. I had slept twelve hours and was still reluctant to get moving. So I did several video chats with family and friends while still snuggled in bed. It felt so good to see their faces, and I imagine it was a relief to them to see mine, as well.

The diarrhea seemed to have been caused by something I ate, as it had subsided. My guess was the boxed coconut milk, which I hadn't been able to refrigerate after opening. I was more concerned about dehydration than nutrients, so I threw away the coconut milk. It was evidently out of my system, hopefully for good.

I texted Dr. Usama to update him that I no longer had diarrhea and was feeling significantly better. Today had been our tentative appointment that we had set two days ago, and I did not feel I needed him to come. It felt as though I was through the worst of the illness. The doctor gave me a call rather than texting me back, which I appreciated greatly. I asked him about next steps, when I could retest to go home, and how that would happen. He told me he had another clinic located inside the airport, which would be closer to my hotel, so he would make arrangements for me to retest there. He said I could take my PCR test again at the ten-day mark, that ten days would likely be the soonest I could hope to receive a negative result. My hope immediately attached itself to being well by day ten. I thought if I could test negative on day ten, I could fly home on day eleven, three whole days early.

The sun was out that morning for the first time since I checked into the hotel. I think the rain was a gift while my COVID-19 symptoms were at their worst. It made it easier to sleep all the time and snuggle in. I took my leftover fruit plate from yesterday's room service order out onto the terrace to get some sun on my face, but a giant bird wanted to join me, and he was not at all scared of me! He got pretty aggressive, and I was not willing to share the food I had, so I took it back inside. After eating, I put on my bathing suit and sat on the terrace in the sun, just soaking it in. It felt so good on my skin. It was the first time I did not feel like I was being held captive since being whisked off the boat five days before.

While I was sitting there on my terrace with my eyes closed, the call to prayer started. What a delicious moment, bathing in the sun and prayer washing over me in waves. I allowed myself to be fully engulfed in the present moment. Just me and the sun and the call to prayer with the waves crashing in the background. I needed this.

I got hot quickly out there in the sun, so I decided to take advantage of the fact that it was not raining and get dressed to walk back to the little corner market. Today was the first day I felt like I had the energy to make it down my stairs and walk the block and a half back to the market. I needed food and water badly. After putting on my street-appropriate clothing, I stepped back out onto my balcony and saw that there was a wall of dark, black clouds moving across the island toward me. I went downstairs and met Sahin near the front door. I pointed up and asked him if it was going to rain.

He giggled melodically, followed by a head bobble. "Not right now!" he answered.

And there it was … another reminder to be fully present. It was indeed *going* to rain, but not just yet. It was not raining right now. I decided to go do what I came outside to do. And if I got wet on the way back, so what? I continued to the market. The man inside handed me a little basket and proceeded to follow me up and down the aisles again. They did not have much available today. I got some Arabian dates, cashews, Happy Cow cheese wedges (I chuckled at the translation, as these are called Laughing Cow at home), and cranberry oat bars, which looked more like crackers or cookies in size and texture. I was hoping to get bananas, but they did not have any. In one of the center aisles, I found shampoo and conditioner, which felt like unwrapping a Wonka chocolate bar and seeing the glimmer of a golden ticket. There was only that watery shower gel in my hotel bathroom—no shampoo or conditioner. My hair felt like frizzy straw! These were my luxury items for the day. I was winning! I carried my groceries and water and shampoo back to my room (still ahead of the rainstorm), and after unpacking them onto my makeshift pantry shelf, I lay down for a little nap. That had been a lot of movement and energy for me.

When I woke up, I went into the bathroom and took a long shower to luxuriously wash and condition my hair. I felt almost giddy! I could not smell the shampoo, which was a strange feeling. You don't realize that you are used to smelling something during certain rote activities until the scent is missing. It left a slightly unsettling gap in the experience. The shampoo felt silky soft and sudsy in my hands, and massaging my scalp felt so nurturing. I was fully immersed in the sensations of hot water pulling the lather out of my hair and down my back, when suddenly the water just stopped. Thankfully, I had nearly finished rinsing the conditioner out. It turned out we only got a certain number of gallons of water to use per room per day, and I had maxed out. What about all the days I hadn't showered? Yeah, no ... those didn't carry over. I think the tank was a certain size, and that was that. Okay then. I would not let this steal my joy at having clean hair. I not only had clean hair but also food and water for dinner tonight. I paused for a moment of gratitude to just let the simplicity of this soak in.

I checked in on my transactions and caught up on my email before going to bed. It was morning for the title companies and real estate agents I was contacting, and they would likely respond, but I would not see those responses until I woke up the next day. It took a full twenty-four hours for us to complete conversations, but at least I was *in* the conversations now.

DAY SIX,
SEPTEMBER 30, 2021

MY AWE GROUP HAD A ZOOM CALL scheduled to begin at 5:30 p.m. Colorado time, 4:30 a.m. in the Maldives. I woke up in time to hop on the call, just ten minutes late thanks to the call to prayer. Seeing all their faces and catching up on what was happening for each of them did my heart good.

We were discussing our inner saboteurs—the ways in which we unconsciously self-sabotage. My top go-to behaviors were to go into hyper-achiever mode and just push through and get it done, or to become restless to the point where I was easily distracted and lacked focus, or to fall into perfectionism where I could be critical of myself and others and legalistic about time and processes. During this call, when asked how my saboteurs were showing up in my current circumstances, I realized that vulnerability had removed them all. Those go-to coping mechanisms simply did not work here. There was no room for them. I could not go into hyper-achiever mode because there was nothing I could work on. I could not go into restless mode without anything available to distract me. And I certainly could not fall prey to my perfectionism ... that realization almost made me snort. There is zero semblance of perfection in this scenario, and if anything, I wanted to break the legalistic rules rather than keep them.

I did not feel as sick that day. I was just dizzy and tired, which were mostly manageable because the bed was my only piece of furniture. I reached out to my friend Karyn to have her look up the metaphysical meaning behind dizziness. She came back with the answer that dizziness is about a refusal to look. Where was I refusing to look? What was I refusing to see? Oh yes, this made so much sense to me. These past few days, I had been afraid to look at this experience, to really engage with my emotions that scared me—the fear, the grief, the anger, the frustration, the powerlessness. I feared these emotions because they felt like they would consume me if I gave them any space. With this new perspective, I consciously decided to release my refusal to look. The mantra suggested for dizziness resonated with me: *I am deeply centered and peaceful in life. It is safe for me to be alive and joyous.* I wrote this in my journal and returned to it again and again to remind myself. It didn't feel true yet, but if I said it enough, maybe it would sink in. *It is safe for me to be alive and joyous.*

I went to make an open-faced peanut butter sandwich and discovered that my remaining bread was moldy. I sat on the edge of my bed holding the bag of moldy bread slices and cried. Hard. I was pretty hungry. I did not have enough food to ever really feel satisfied, and bread was the one thing that had come close to satiating me. And on the heels of having just thrown out the coconut milk, my food pantry was quite bleak. My grief over this loss made me realize that I was not just hungry for food. I was hungry. Full stop. I hungered for *all* that nourishes us: for companionship, for support, for love, for human touch, for a sense of safety, for stability.

I ate a cheese wedge and five dates, but when did that ever fill someone up? I could not do anything about the bread or my hunger, physical or emotional, so I decided I was going to break quarantine for something that

I would not have considered a necessity in the same way as food and water until today. My mental health needed some space to breathe, and that was worth breaking a rule or two. I needed to get out of this room and walk, to get some fresh air and sunshine without carrying heavy bags or wearing a mask. The beach across the street was calling to me. The locals came out to enjoy it in the evenings when it cooled off, but in the mornings and the heat of the middle of the day it had been completely empty, which made it feel like a safe option.

I did not even try to cover up this time. It was too hot, and with the beach being empty, I decided it would be okay. I put on a pair of shorts and a tank top, walked across the cobblestone street, and stepped into the sand for the first time. There was a grove of trees in a long row right next to the street, growing in the sand. I had seen these trees from my balcony every day, and now I was standing underneath them in their shade. I heard the rustle of their leaves in the breeze. I kicked off my flip-flops and walked through the trees onto the beach. There, right in my path just a few yards away, was a short log lying on its side meant to be used for seating. The sun was hitting it just perfectly, almost as if it were in a spotlight. It was facing the sea. I knew, just really knew, it was for me. This was mine. I felt it in my soul that I would sit there and ponder life and talk with the Sea. This would be my spot while I was here.

I sat down for a while and just enjoyed the view. The Indian Ocean was right in front of me, a gorgeous, clear, turquoise-colored water reflecting gold sunlight. The soft, beige sand was hot and warm between my toes. My skin was still brown from my time on the boat and glistened with sweat and looked pretty. There was a barrier reef a little way out, so the waves were more turbulent up against it, but in front of the barrier the water was quieter and calm as it moved toward the beach. I imagined that the people on this island probably built that reef to create a swim beach, and perhaps to protect the beach from erosion since it was quite a narrow strip of sand between the street and the water. I stood up and walked to the edge of the surf and put my feet in the ocean. This was exactly what I needed. It was grounding. I was back in my own body. I felt calmer and reassured that I was okay. *It was safe for me to be alive and joyous.*

I MET ME BY THE SEA

by Janine Valentine

We first connected
Before my memories begin
The essence of you
Breathing beneath my skin.
Rising and falling,
Shallow and deep,
Rhythmically inspired
Expansion and release.
Present long before my arrival
And long after my eventual decline,
Inspiring and supporting
With freedom to define.
One Source
All connected
Eternally Divine.

I am grateful
For the life lessons you taught
Along the way.
How you retreat
Twice a day,
Exposing tide pools
Filled with starfish and anemone
Developing my imagination
And curiosity,

And even bravery,
As I explored as far in
As you would allow
Inside your home
While you were out ...
Seeking to know more deeply
What you were about.
Upon your return
Your edges lapped at my shins
My awakeness
And numbing
Co-exist.
As you rush to greet me
Your embrace,
Bracingly cold.
Feeling your presence
Intense and bold
Then, the emotions of our reunion
Quickly submerged,
As numbness
Takes hold.

I build sandcastles along the shore
Meticulously,
As you teach
That creation,
No matter the effort
Or beauty,
Is all temporary.
I can resist

And try to save it
Or submit to your changes
By offering it up as a gift.
Sometimes you soften the edges
Before erasing it,
Sometimes swiftly
And catastrophically
Reclaiming it.

You also deposit treasures
At my feet.
Driftwood sculptures
And tangled seaweed,
Translucent agates
And tumbled sea glass.
Their turbulent journey
Leading to this moment
Of discovery.
Fragile sand dollars
Sometimes miraculously intact,
Having survived
The impact.
Others broken in half
Freeing the skeletal bird inside
Proving that even after
Catastrophic breaks
That which we hide within
Is actually designed
To help us fly.
Perhaps my attraction

To collecting seashells
Is a nod of recognition
To the discarded carcasses
And outgrown shelters —
Nostalgic remnants
From where we have come,
Providing contrast
Against what we have Become.

I learned to dance and twirl
Within your waves
And how to let go
And float
When stillness is craved.
Floating on your surface
I get a glimpse inside
The world within
Hidden from sight.
Disarmed as I experience
Where my fear
And truth
Collide.
Instinctively guided
As the tide rises
And falls.
Cradled in your arms
Swaying gently side-to-side
I experience your maternal instincts
As you rock me to sleep.

I learned to scream
Under cover of your turbulent roar.
And to never turn my back
In the presence of Power.
For deep below
May lie a violent undertow
With a malevolent intention
Of taking me
In another direction.
Just as with my own
Shadow self,
There is a wildness
Under your surface
Behind curtains of kelp,
A hint of danger
As we glimpse our Purpose.

Communing with you
Is my sacred space.
Your saltwater
From the same Source
As the tears on my face.
You interconnect the entire globe
We have much to learn
From all that you hold.
It is such a comfort
To meet along the shore
Returning to home
My Truth restored.

I reluctantly walked back across the street to come up to my room. I was not anxious to return to my little room, but I knew I needed to rest again. I crossed the street just a few steps south of where I had entered the beach and landed on the sidewalk in front of the restaurant next-door to my hotel—the one that provided room service. It was just an open-air store front, really, with a glass counter showcasing pastries and a cash register next to a cooler with cold juices, sodas, and water. I could see into the back through an open door where there was a guy working in the kitchen. The sign above read The Chill Café. The name struck me as cute, given that this was not an English-speaking island.

The man standing out front caught my eye and spoke to me. He asked if I was the one staying at the hotel next door. I think this was an easy assumption since there were no other tourists around this area. He had very good English and asked me why I had not ordered more room service from him. I explained that I did not have very much cash with me, and since he accepted only cash payment, I could not eat there. He was surprised I would be staying such a long time and said that he would accept my credit card because of the length of my stay. Woo-hooooo! Elation flooded my body! I placed an order right then and there: *two* entrees, Nasi Goreng and Tuna Mas Huni with Roshi, and two big bottles of water. Tuna Mas Huni with Roshi is the traditional Maldivian breakfast, tuna with coconut and lime served with a side of bread similar to pita, and I fell in love with it on the boat. It was familiar. Nasi Goreng is what I had ordered with the last of my cash—basically a fried rice dish served with a fried egg on top.

I told him I would be right back with my credit card and to pick up my food. He said no; he would speak to the men that run my hotel and tell them he had authorized me to use a credit card during my stay. He would send them up with my food when it was ready, and they could bring my card down to him to pay at that time. I could have hugged him with delight! But of course, I did not. While my symptoms had diminished, I knew I did still have COVID, not to mention that I was a woman wearing a tank top and shorts on the street speaking to a man. None of this was appropriate. I quietly and sincerely thanked him and walked up my stairs to my room to wait for my feast.

About thirty minutes later, Sahin brought me a tray bursting with fresh and beautifully plated foods. There was a large glass of fresh-squeezed orange juice that I could not taste at all but was still happiness in a glass. The color was vibrant orange with a fresh orange wedge on the rim and an eco-friendly metal straw, which also delighted me. I could feel the tanginess of the juice in my mouth, and I imagined the vitamin C spreading throughout my body to aid in my healing. In the lack of taste and smell, there was opportunity to discover new ways to enjoy what I had. I could feel tingles from tangy or heat from spicy in my mouth. I was aware of temperature and texture and found comfort in them. I sent gratitude to the hands that prepared this food and those that delivered it to my room.

There are gifts inside the things we fear. Always. I was beginning to hear the Universe whispering to me that day to find the gifts. So I gave that some thought and decided to journal an actual list of them.

There were gifts that happened before I even got there that were helping me now—for example, the pet sitter I chose. I had moved just prior to this trip and had to find a new pet sitter. The first one I interviewed was really great but had wanted to watch my dogs at her home instead of mine, which was understandable and I was open to it, but my preference was that my girls (that's how I refer to my dogs) stayed in our home where things were familiar while I was gone because they were used to me being with them pretty much all the time. It felt like a new environment might be more stressful to them. So I kept looking and hired the one who was still there with them in my home. The first pet sitter would not have been able to extend her stay two more weeks, but this one did. I was so grateful for the comfort that gave me.

I also trained my assistants to help my clients a bit during my vacation. I had never done this before. Usually, my clients just made do without me for seven-to-ten days once a year, and I made it up on the back end when I got home. But this time, I spent the month prior to leaving teaching my assistants how to help with certain things. And now that I was going to be gone a full month, I was grateful that we took the time to prepare them to help in this way.

I randomly bought that box of Mucinex day/night combo capsules the day before flying out. This was the only thing I had available to help with my symptoms, and while there were not enough capsules for me to take full doses, or even at regular intervals, it had still provided relief and was exactly the right thing to have with me. I had never traveled with cold medicine before.

Wendy left me her cash. Even though only ten dollars of it was useable there, it was ten more dollars than I had, and that made a difference in my fear mindset and had allowed me to purchase food and water.

Also, Wendy stayed with me during the scariest first part of getting the news and getting retested and waiting all those hours contemplating all the worst things. What a gift to not have to be alone during those first hours.

I picked this hotel blindly and very quickly while in shock and trauma, and while I did not see it during the first twenty-four hours, it had truly been perfect in so many ways. This balcony. My view of the beach and sea. The sunrises. The mosque right next door, gifting me with five calls to prayer every day. A desk to work from when I felt well enough.

And now I could add that the owner of the restaurant next door granted me permission to use my credit card so I could have healthy prepared meals delivered to my room.

I had so many friends and family members reaching out to me via WhatsApp every day, early in the morning (which is nighttime for them) and then just before I fell asleep (as they were just waking up). I was loved and on their minds. This was a gift.

And there were the small moments of joy that immersed me in the present moment, such as the sun on my face, my feet in the surf, the log bench

I found facing the sea, shampooing my hair, and the tingle in my mouth from fresh-squeezed orange juice. All these seemingly little things that held me in the now (even if only for a few minutes) were incredible gifts. Being truly present was an elusive concept under these circumstances, as my mind insisted on worrying over the next minute, hour, day and reliving the many hard moments that had happened that I hadn't yet been able to process.

There's a difference between trying to be grateful to put a positive spin on what was happening in an attempt to convince myself that I was okay, and just noticing and being present with these tiny joys and unexpected beauty within all this hard stuff. I was awakening to the odd sensation of pleasure intertwined with my pain. Not escapism or idealism. Just being with the entirety of what was true, rather than seeing only what was not going the way I wanted it to.

All these gifts were reiterating the message that I am loved, my higher power had not forgotten me—not for one moment—and I could trust myself, my instincts, my intuition, and my Source. The spiritual care I was receiving had been so incredibly personalized to what my needs were, the things I specifically needed to feel comforted. I could choose to blame my higher power for allowing this scary, horrible thing to happen to me, or I could choose to see my higher power's care, nurturing, and protection throughout. It was me who was assigning the label that this whole situation was "bad." Perhaps I needed to reframe my perspective. Perhaps the gifts and the beauty inside the fear *are* the point. I'm just not sure how to get there.

That afternoon, I decided to request a change of my sheets and fresh towels, which I did when Sahin came back up to clear away my dishes. The sheets were far from fresh after I had basically lived on that bed for six days, eating on it, and lying on it all sweaty. And the towels … well, those had been through my learning curve on the toilet system. I felt guilty asking Sahin to be inside my room, knowing it was contaminated from my illness. I hoped I might be far enough through my symptoms that he would be okay. This was the other "rule" that I felt I needed to break today for my overall wellness. The two men working at the hotel always wore their masks, and I wore mine while in their presence. Sahin arrived carrying fresh sheets and towels, along with a broom and some cleaning supplies. I was going to get the full cleaning service! I stepped out of my room onto the balcony while he remade my bed, cleaned the bathroom, and swept the floor.

When he was finished, I handed him my last $2 cash (aside from the $15 I had set aside for my taxi back and forth for testing and to get to the airport). I was more okay releasing the last of my cash now that I had access to restaurant food and water with my credit card. Besides, I could not in good conscience withhold this tip from him. He had just cleaned my room, unaware that it was a COVID recovery den. He left the sliding door open the whole time he was in there, but he was changing my sheets and cleaning the bathroom. It was a fair amount of work and potential exposure. I realized that $2 was not nearly enough, and yet it was everything I had, which made it feel meaningful to me. I handed it to him with both emotions present—shame at it not being enough and proud of myself for having the courage to give away my last two dollars. The economy there is different, so it felt like more to him than it did to me, and he graciously accepted it and thanked me with a small bow and a smile. He then lingered and chatted with me on the balcony from a safe distance for a few minutes. Our conversation was hilarious.

I asked where he was from.

"Bangladesh."

I asked his age.

"Twenty-five."

He wondered why I was alone. He asked if I was married.

"Not anymore."

He told me he thought I should be married, and then offered to find me a man while I was staying there. He said he knew many single men, and that

I was so beautiful I should be a wife. He was so sincere and had such kind and genuine intentions that I managed to stifle my laughter.

"No, thank you. I like being alone right now. Maybe someday I will have a husband again."

He shook his head, confused by me and my crazy western ways. I thanked him for changing my sheets and went back inside.

I tried to call my trip insurance company. I did buy a policy for this trip, but I had no idea what it might cover for this situation. I figured the company's representatives would probably at least advocate for me while I was here, should I need something, and also assist with rebooking my flights home. It turned out the company did not have a toll-free number from this country, and I sat on a very expensive hold for several minutes before giving up. Instead, I called my sister, and she kindly offered to call the company for me. She reached someone there and texted me back a few hours later to tell me that the company would not do anything for me from there. Once I got home, I could submit my claim and staff would determine, what (if anything) would be covered and reimbursed. No help up front. Good to know, and also annoying.

There also was no way for me to call the airline regarding my flight home without paying a lot of money for the call. Just like with my trip insurance company, there was no toll-free number for the airline that I could use from where I was. I had never needed to use a toll-free number in another country where it just wasn't an option. Who knew that these numbers worked only from certain places? How were we to get help from countries that were not covered? I messaged my friend Jenny, a frequent traveler, and she called American Airlines for me. She found out that I would have to pay only any difference in airfare once I was ready to rebook my ticket. They were giving me full credit for the flight I missed and not charging me a change fee due to the circumstances. I was thrilled. I had been unable to alert the airlines that I was going to miss my flight, and it had been several days already. I figured that ticket and the money used to buy it were long gone. What wonderful news this was! The airline made note in my file and would allow Jenny to rebook my ticket for me when we were ready. This was such a relief to have this big piece ready to go once I was allowed to leave.

I had not yet napped. It was now 5:00 p.m., and I was exhausted. I took one of my precious ibuprofens because my neck and the base of my skull were really sore. I didn't care what time it was, I was going to sleep early for sure. I had fresh sheets on my king-size bed, and they felt unbelievably good as I slipped in.

DAY SEVEN,
OCTOBER 1, 2021

I WAS ALREADY A LITTLE AWAKE, lying in the dark, as the 4:40 a.m. call to prayer began. It felt as though two arms were reaching inside me and gently lifting my heart up above my body as an offering of gratitude to Source. It was so soothing to my soul, and certainly no accident that I landed at this hotel right next to the only mosque in Hulhumalé. It had been, and would continue to be, a daily reminder to be grateful.

I was tired and achy again today and did not want to get out of bed. My ears and glands felt full, lots of pressure, and I was *so* tired. Perhaps I overdid it yesterday with my short walk to the beach. I decided to just let my body have what it needed. This was a new concept for me. Pretty much all my life I had made my body just go along for the ride of whatever the day held. My body was clearly telling me it needed my attention. It needed sleep for sure, but I wondered what else. I asked it, and the answer surprised me. I wanted to hear the vibration of my love tuner. A love tuner is like a small whistle on a string that when blown makes a sound that resonates at 528 Hz, which is the frequency of the emotion of love. I messaged Kelly, a friend and AWE sister who also had a love tuner, and requested a recording of its sound, which she sent to me within minutes. I played it over and over several times, letting it wash over me. *I am loved. I am loving. I am love.*

It was rainy again, and it was comforting. It felt sleepy like me, and cleansing. Rest and release. I shall mimic the rain.

While I was lying there, my brother Todd called me via WhatsApp for the first time. He told me with absolute certainty that I was going to test negative and be on that flight home next Friday. It was not just his words that comforted me but the way he said them with such calm confidence; he wasn't trying hard to convince me or himself. It wasn't a brave face he was putting on. His demeanor left no room but for it to be true, and part of me was able to believe him. As an adult, I have learned there's something about my siblings that is stabilizing. We've known each other our whole lives, and there's a trust there unlike any other. We three have a deep friendship and love for one another, and we're good about reaching out to restore balance for each other when needed. Todd's voice on the phone did that for me that day from the other side of the world. Powerful.

As I sat down to my computer to check on work files, I sipped some ginger tea that I had ordered with my breakfast. It had large chunks of fresh ginger in it, and was visibly quite strong. It was such an odd sensation to feel the bitterness of it physically on my tongue but not taste or smell it at all. I have realized that I can *feel* the taste of certain foods. I had never noticed this aspect of food before.

I glanced at my emails and had the sudden realization that it was the first day of October. I left home in mid-September, but it had still felt like summer at home and the pool still had been open. I would return to the autumn in mid-October. Time warp.

The phone in my room was not working. Rubel and Sahin could not figure out why. So to order room service, I had to suit up (put on appropriate clothing and a bra and a face mask) and walk down the long, steep spiral staircase to put in my order at the front desk. This sort of defeated the purpose of "room service." I would have to do this twice that day. Scratch that. I *got* to do this twice that day. Because room service, no matter how inconvenient, was now an option for me! But it did take everything I had energetically to make it down and back up, get lots of rest in between, and then do it again later in the day. On that day's menu: a continental breakfast plate consisting of two slices of toast, one fried egg, and some apple and orange slices, and then later in the day, I ordered Maldivian Style Noodles, which reminded me of ramen noodles with seafood mixed in.

On my first trip downstairs, I came across a dinosaur of a praying mantis on the wall right at my face height that I ended up passing all four times. My friends all know this about me, but I should let you in on it: I am not very outdoorsy. I enjoy being *in* nature very much, but do not like to get nature *on* me. Bugs, no matter how "friendly," are not anything I choose to get near. "Oh good—you're still here!" I exclaimed to the praying mantis on my return trip. "Let's keep it that way. Do not move right now, please!" I implored, and then I slipped past.

I kept picturing the made-for-TV movie of this experience, which also was helping me find the humor in the ridiculous, such as traipsing all the way down an enormous spiral staircase while dizzy and exhausted to order what we were still ironically referring to as room service. It truly was funny if you could step back and be the observer instead of the one fighting to make it down the stairs without falling (or having a praying mantis jump on you) to get some food so you would have the energy you would need a few hours later to do it again.

I sent my daughter a photo of the log on the beach that I sat on the day before. She texted me back to excitedly tell me that *Rogue One* was filmed on that beach. She and her husband were quite excited about me getting to be on this beach, as they are huge Star Wars fans. I have never seen the movie, but I made a note to watch it sometime and see if the beach looked familiar. I guess while I was picturing myself in a tragic drama/comedy movie, they were imagining me in a sci-fi movie scene! Somehow that also felt accurate.

I made a typo on a text to my mom. I meant to type: "Mostly I was on my bed today ... tired and no place else to be with the terrace not an option due to rain." But instead it read "Mostly a wad on my bed today ...," which I found hilarious. I laughed and laughed, and read it again and laughed some more. The typo felt oddly appropriate. I did feel like a wad on my bed. Somewhere inside myself I realized this was not as funny as my reaction indicated. I was laughing a bit like a crazy person over this. I had a brief flash when I wondered if I might be losing it. Was my sanity teetering on the edge? And then I decided I really didn't care, because it felt so good to just laugh. I needed that. *I am hilarious company for myself, and I am all I have at the moment, so let's just roll with it!*

It was bedtime at that point, so I texted with my mom and sister in a group thread that my sister had created for the three of us. After catching them up on my day, the conversation ended like this:

My sister: Sweet, happy dreams to you, honey. You are a warrior.

My mom: Good night from the warrior's mom.

This may be my favorite text message ever.

DAY EIGHT,
OCTOBER 2, 2021

IT WAS SATURDAY AGAIN. I was looping around into another week. Time was indeed passing.

It had rained all night, which was a lovely soundtrack and also cooling. I slept ten hours, so that was good. I still felt sleepy and was moving slowly.

I grounded myself to the planet that morning by reminding myself that home and that hotel are on the same literal and physical sphere. That was comforting. Home could start to feel really far away if I let it. But we all stand upon the same earth. This is probably a great perspective for all of humanity to be reminded of. Our connection to one another is undeniable. We inhabit the same planet. It is a closed system. We cannot be truly alone even if we want to be.

I went downstairs and ordered a fresh fruit plate, along with another order of Tuna Mas Huni, the traditional Maldivian breakfast. I imagined I would learn to make this at home, as I had become quite fond of it. The day ahead already felt long, and I lacked the motivation or energy it seemed to need from me. I was struggling already this morning. I felt sluggish, even though my COVID symptoms were improving. My body was doing a lot of hard healing work and processing stress, so regardless of having COVID, being tired was to be expected. My mind was my bigger challenge that day. I felt sad and weepy, and the morning was just crawling by. I kept creeping toward anxiety about retesting and getting home and had to consciously attempt to pull myself back into positive thinking.

I tried doing a Qi Gong video designed to boost the immune system and tonify the lungs. My friend Genevieve had sent me the link. It was only twenty minutes long, and I could do it standing in the small space next to my bed. It did not require me to sit or lie down, something I would never do on that floor because I was too skittish about the bugs, even post-spraying. I never did see that beetle again from the first night, but I was aware he might still be my roommate. I did get a bit sweaty from the movement even though it was far from aerobic. This reminded me that I was still recovering from something that was a very big deal to my body. I found compassion for my tired, sluggish self. It did feel good to do something, and I moved some energy in and out, which felt important. And that could be enough for now. *Good work, Janine.*

A few months before, during some time of self-reflection, it occurred to me that I had been avoiding physical activity because I was avoiding feeling a lot of heavy emotions. I had thought I just didn't have the energy to go for a walk or do yoga because I was weighed down with sadness and grief, but the truth was that it was an avoidance of feeling the feelings. What I noticed when I did force myself outside for that walk was that the emotions rose up and out. An outcome of physical exercise was that it increased my awareness and expression of my thoughts and emotions. The mind-body-spirit connection is real, and moving my body is key.

It occurred to me now that I could actually eliminate and banish fear via movement of my body. Wow! I felt like I had just discovered gravity. This was a huge paradigm shift. While I had known that moving our bodies is good for our bodies, and that it could even clear the mind, I had still given myself a pass on doing my workouts or going for walks when I was feeling anything overwhelming like sadness, anger, stress, or exhaustion. Honestly, I was in those states more often than I wasn't over the past couple of years, thanks to the pandemic and all the horrible things going on in our country, as well as the passing of my dad. I now understood that these emotions were literally energy-in-motion and needed to be moved through and *out* of my body. By ignoring them or literally just sitting in them, I was giving those emotions a permanent home inside my body that would continue to affect me long after my conscious awareness of them passed. I had the power to help myself heal if only I would do what felt counterintuitive: move. My body actually wanted to move. It was an old, unhealthy coping mechanism in myself that was afraid of allowing these less-than-desirable (and therefore, uncomfortable) emotions to be expressed, and I instinctively avoided things that might cause them to slip out ... like moving my body. This new understanding felt powerful. Empowering. I was taking my power back.

I decided to put this new knowledge to good use. I got dressed and walked back to the market to refresh my snack pantry. Even though I was now able to order room service, it required going downstairs followed by a wait time while the restaurant prepared and delivered it. Sometimes I just wanted a little something more immediate while I stayed in bed. I seemed to have found a rhythm of ordering two room service meals a day, with all my water for the day in the first order each morning, and then filling in around those with whatever I had left from the market. I never ordered both of my meals for the day at the same time. I preferred to not set a plan in place for a specific time for that second meal, which was such an interesting change in my way of being. I typically loved a plan and a schedule. But not there. Needing to remember that food was arriving at a certain time felt like a lot of work and an imposition on the very little bit of freedom I had. What if I wanted to walk the beach or take a shower? What if I needed a nap? I wanted zero restrictions on the few options I had open to me, so the cost of that was an extra trip downstairs each day to place my meal order. Thus, the little snacks from the corner market provided the flexibility I craved.

I enjoyed my walk there and back very much. It was Saturday, and the community was out. It was not crowded by any means, but there were people on the beach and on the street. I felt like I was part of the community. The market clerk guy smiled at me in recognition. On this third trip to the market, I knew where things were, and I moved about with more purpose and intention. He still followed right beside me, but we were a team now—him reaching for the things up high that I pointed to and the two of us smiling at one another in lieu of conversation.

I stopped by my little restaurant next door to place a dinner order of tuna kabobs with a salad before heading upstairs with my grocery bags. Upon reaching my terrace, I noticed that there was now a couple staying in the room next door, so the terrace was being shared once again. I asked about their reservation later at the front desk and learned they were there for two nights. Sigh. It's funny that I lamented being alone and then I was annoyed when I was not alone up there in my high tower. Interacting with other travelers and locals was one of my favorite things about traveling, especially in other cultures. Knowing it was potentially unsafe for this couple if I were to join them, even in a mask on an open-air terrace, was a loss of an opportunity for me. I imagined the conversation we might have had under other circumstances, broken English heavily supplemented with body language. Also true was that in this contagious state I felt more vulnerable. My aloneness was more comforting to me than I had realized. Perhaps solitude was addictive, and I had begun to crave it. Nevertheless, my world got smaller, confined to this tiny room as long as there were others staying next door.

The initial urgency of the physical aspects of finding a safe place to quarantine, getting access to medical care if needed, having food and water available, and coping with my body's reaction and symptoms from both

COVID and adrenaline was waning. With my physical safety now in check, I found that my body, mind, and spirit were turning full time to face my Big Fear—my aloneness. It was time for my nonphysical healing, the reason I had likely been brought there by the Universe. I was still in resistance to looking at this, but I had no choice. The Universe was being quite clear with me, bringing my aloneness and my suppression of my emotions into my awareness over and over. It was uncomfortable.

There comes a point in every challenging situation when resisting what just *is* becomes futile. I had reached that moment. There I was, stuck there alone. No amount of railing against it would change that. Nothing could change my circumstances. So my work was to make peace with it and maybe even find *joy* there. There was joy in the sunrise, and in the call to prayer. There was bound to be more.

I decided I would return to my log bench on the beach rather than burrowing into my bed watching another endless movie marathon. As the words of my mom and sister from the previous night calling me a warrior echoed in my head, I found myself referring to this bench in my thoughts as my Warrior Bench. I did not yet know that the name would stick, but it did. It was now and forever my Warrior Bench.

After making the trek, I took a seat on my Warrior Bench and noticed that up the beach a little way there was a group of women in full burkas swimming in the sea. They each held onto a foam swim noodle. I speculated that the noodles were probably to keep them afloat with all that heavy fabric weighing them down, at serious risk of being dragged under the surface. It looked like a group swimming lesson, with some women lying on the edge of the surf practicing their kicking there in the shallow water. There was a man with them who remained on the beach, sitting in the shade of the trees a little way back from the water but still watching them protectively. I surreptitiously took a couple of photos with my phone. I didn't want to be obvious about it, and yet I wanted to remember this and to be able to show this photo to my friends at home. It was such a contrast to the western swimsuits I was accustomed to. And yet it was also just women playing in the sea, enjoying each other's company. This scene playing out in front of me took the day's conversation with the Sea in a new direction. There was clearly a deep metaphor here.

The Sea is feminine. Water suppresses fire. I am an Aries—a fire sign. There I was on an island surrounded by the feminine Sea with a population that was predominantly Muslim. There were these women wearing burkas—some even still had on their black gloves—bobbing up and down with the waves. All around me was evidence of the suppression of the feminine in our physical world, as well as the divine feminine. Inside of me were what I was beginning to recognize as scars from the suppression of my own feminine nature. In the past, I had felt safer working in the logical, focused, goal-driven, independent energies associated with the masculine side of our nature, and I suppressed what I perceived to be my less acceptable feminine energies of emotions, intuition, receiving, and collaboration. I had been working on finding the balance and harmony between my masculine and feminine sides for over a year. Writing had played a big part in helping me express my emotions in creative ways and opening up to my intuition. In a big-picture view of this swimming lesson that was taking place in front of me, I could see a suppression of the feminine in most countries in the world. Women are often treated as less than, expected to hide our true nature and strength under heavy layers of saturated fabric. It was presented as safer for us to be anonymous, status quo, and homogenous, than it was to stand out as unique. I once again watched those women swimming in front of me and imagined how I would feel if I were one of them. The weight of the clothing was palpable and familiar, for I too have worn many heavy layers of peoples' expectations that did not belong to me, as well as my own fears that held me down. I imagined stripping off the burka in the sea and letting it drift quietly to the ocean floor, the touch of the water now against my bare skin, the vulnerability and risk of my nakedness in the water making me seem smaller, and also more visible, the thrill of my newfound freedom of movement, the unfamiliar buoyancy at the removal of my very real fear of being pulled under and drowning without an identity.

For the past several years, I had pictured my life journey as a river. I had used the image to help me with the idea of staying in flow, of relaxing into what was actually happening, even when it might be a class 5 section of whitewater. Suddenly, I had an image of the Universe dropping a colossal cement dam into my river, purposely choosing a spot around a curve so I would not see it coming, and then placing some haphazardly scattered red flags along the way that I may or may not have seen before hitting this new wall, my face smooshed up against it briefly until the momentum of the current swooshed me off to the right, onto a whole new path. We were forging a new river. I had become used to going around some big boulders in my riverbed. I had even put some of them there myself. But diverting my riverbed path in a whole new direction? I did not see this coming. And yet … the best thing to do was to stop resisting it and flailing around, throwing a tantrum in this water, going on about how alone I was, because I was indeed alone, and I could drown if I didn't chill the fuck out.

I remember when I was first learning to swim I was taught if I felt too tired to swim anymore, to just flip onto my back and float. *Well, Janine, it is time to flip onto your back and float* … total surrender and trust. I was traveling through foreign lands, both physically and spiritually. I might as well enjoy the views (both the literal views out my window there in the Maldives and the spiritual perspectives). They were all new to me, and without a doubt, a gift. As a lifelong compulsive planner who needed the perception that I was in control, surrender used to feel like giving up, conceding, submitting out of a sense of "I should," and settling for what was, even though it wasn't what I had wanted. This surrender that I was experiencing now felt so different. It felt like relief, peace, stillness, light. It was genuinely like floating on my back

BOTH THINGS ARE TRUE

in the waves, becoming one with the One who had designed this moment for me, leaning into trust and letting go of the splashing around and resisting. It did not feel at all like I was settling. This was far better than what I would be doing "for" myself, which ironically would be "against" myself. This new perspective helped me realize that planning was my gateway drug back to creating structure that bound me as if it were the law, holding me hostage to myself and all caged up. Surrendering to what was, was freedom.

This was a new version of surrender. I was finding true acceptance. Once I accepted whatever was happening, it grafted me into the present moment rather than where fear lived in the thoughts of past and future. I recalled a mantra shared with me by my coach, Cynthia: "Be with where you are." I know that looks like a typo at first glance, so re-read it: "Be *with* where you are." Yes. I was here. *Here.* It just was what it was. I needed to be here with myself and not abandon myself. My survival required it. My mental health required it. My day-to-day life felt like an active awake meditation. Just like when I meditated at home, seated, with my eyes closed, and my mind wandered to my to-do list, I simply returned my attention to my breathing. I would consciously bring myself fully present in each moment. Only now, here, I was doing this all day long as my mind wandered to problem-solving things that had not even happened yet, trying to get in front of my fears and get myself home. I consciously returned to my breath, to what I was doing in that moment physically. I told myself, often aloud, things such as "Today is Thursday. I am lying on my bed in the Maldives, and my body is actively healing itself even in this moment." Those thoughts kept me grounded in the present, sticking to what was actually happening right then, not what had happened or what might happen next. This mantra stayed with me the remainder of my time on the island and well beyond. I would get it tattooed on my arm months after my return home, because I never again wanted to forget to be present with myself. Life is too short to abandon ourselves in favor of the past or the unforeseeable future. I did not want to miss all the joy!

This experience had already profoundly changed me. I was facing my greatest fear, just like I had to do during my divorce eight years earlier, only this time I *knew* it held gifts for me that I could not yet see or even imagine, that all of this would eventually be a good thing, that this happened *for* me in the end. Leaning in and trusting that this time around with this life lesson had allowed me to get to this headspace of trust and appreciation more quickly. After about a week of marinating in dark fear, I was grateful. Deeply grateful. Quarantined in this room in the Maldives, I could now see the stark reality of the fear I had lived with my whole life and how it had constricted me. I had covered myself in layer after layer of fear as if it were a heavy dark burka, shrouding my possibilities behind layers that both protected and limited me. As long as my fear was the dominant force, the protection had mattered more than the limitations that came alongside it. I had made myself smaller and less-than to avoid being seen, out of fear of the consequences of disapproval and rejection. Over the past year or two, I had practiced choosing to move through some of my fears, dropping the protective layers to practice vulnerability. I had become willing to be seen by others. No more safe anonymity. And now, the Universe had decided I was ready to face my Big Fear of being truly alone, of having only myself to lean on and trust, of fearing that I would not be capable or be enough. Coming out and being seen as I truly am to *myself* had been harder than it was to do with others. I hadn't minded sharing my insecurity or weakness with friends who could then help me or do that thing with me (or even for me). Being vulnerable in that way served a purpose. There on that island, I was just with me. I could not rely on anyone else to help me, reflect back to me, define me, set boundaries for me, or make choices for me. My raw vulnerability just sat there with me. No rescue was on its way. I had to be enough because I was all I was going to get. Going deep inside this fear was setting me free. It was that uncomfortable kind of freedom, where the animal that has known only its cage steps outside and then turns back toward the cage thinking it holds comfort. But my cage had been stolen unceremoniously from this beach, as soon as I had stepped out of it to explore. The Sea sent a series of gentle waves to quietly pull it out to the deep, beyond retrieval. Just as the weight of my figurative layers of burka cloth had felt familiar while also weighing me down, that cage had felt comfortable while keeping me small. I looked out across the sea in front of me and imagined that I saw one last glint of sunlight off the metal bars just before my cage went under, never to be seen again. The things that had hidden me from the world and myself had been buried at sea. I was free. It was time to find my new edges.

DAY NINE,
OCTOBER 3, 2021

UPON WAKING, I walked downstairs to order an early breakfast and a ginger tea, only to learn that apparently we were all locked inside this place at night. I was grateful I had no idea until now because that made me feel claustrophobic and brought up all kinds of questions about why we were locked in. Was it unsafe out there at night? What if there was a fire? But there was a padlock on the door on the inside, so either Sahin or Rubel must be there with us somewhere. I went back upstairs and waited about an hour and then walked all the way back downstairs to try again. The door had been opened. Relief washed over me. I decided to walk across the street to sit on the beach for a bit.

I went straight to my Warrior Bench and had a long chat with the Universe. I called in all my angels, guardians, guides, and my higher power to go in front of me and clear the path of any and all obstacles to getting me home quickly and smoothly. I envisioned a negative COVID test coming to me in just a few days, and then I would be booked on the next available flight and board with no issues in my paperwork or otherwise. As I sat in silence and watched the Sea, I was aware that in this moment I felt both peace and power. I had a deep discussion with the Sea regarding this duality of peace and power. That visual of the Sea in front of me, turbulent outside the man-made barrier, and smooth and calm inside it, was a helpful image to apply to my own soul and circumstances. I had a tangible example in front of me that turbulence and calm can and do coexist. It was not one or the other. Both things are true simultaneously. The barriers (or even perceived barriers) were man-made. I recognized that I had full access to divine peace and divine power simultaneously as well—just like the Sea. I claimed these and bathed myself in them, absorbing, purifying, becoming. *And so it is.*

I headed back to my room, stopping to place my order for breakfast, including hot ginger tea and fresh-squeezed juice, before climbing the stairs. Back in my room, I was immediately bored. What now? And then I realized that it was a privilege to be bored. It meant I was feeling better! When I was really sick, I was not bored because I was sleeping and surviving. I took boredom as a wonderful sign that I was healing!

I bit into a leftover slice of apple from the fruit plate I ordered the day before, and ... I could *taste* it! It was the first thing I had tasted in over a week. I was so excited by this that I snapped a photo of myself being excited while eating my apple slice and sent the photo to almost everyone I was connected with via WhatsApp back home. It was the middle of the night there, and I would not see any responses until the next morning, but I wanted to share my victory and my happiness. I wondered if they would be able to relate to how happy tasting an apple could be. Pure joy!

Most everyone had been wondering who I got this virus from and commenting on how strange it was that only two people on the whole boat tested positive. They speculated that there almost certainly had to be a crew member who had it. From my perspective, it really did not matter. We cannot undo it. No one gave this to me on purpose. We all took precautions and everyone on that boat, guests and crew alike, had tested negative before we set sail. This was a perfect example of how random this virus can be. My roommate had not gotten it. The husband of the Russian woman who tested positive had not gotten it. None of the eleven friends traveling with me ended up testing positive even upon returning home. I had just lost (or won?) the COVID lottery. And I know it happened for a reason. I needed a time out so Source could have my full attention. We had important work to do.

I got a surprise WhatsApp message from the bartender on the boat. He and one of the guys from the housekeeping crew were staying at a hotel in Hulhumalé also. They were on a few days' break. I looked up their hotel on Google Maps and discovered it was only a ten-minute walk south of me. When I told him where I was, we could not believe how close we were, and he texted back that they were leaving right away to walk toward me. They invited me to do the same, and we would have coffee. I felt *alive*. I would get to be with familiar people again! Even though this was someone I had known for only a week, he felt like the closest thing to family I had right now. We found an adorable little open-air café with murals of flowers on the walls, and he bought me a coffee. We lingered long enough to have a second cup. The three of us talked of our home lives, comparing cultures and finding a deeper understanding of each other, even with our language barrier. I nearly skipped back to my hotel with happiness!

Fifty-two stairs from the lobby of the hotel to my room. I finally counted them that day on my way back up. I knew it was a lot, and I wanted to know exactly how many for when I told these stories to my friends and family back home. Even I was surprised by the number. I did, however, notice that I was not as winded anymore by the time I got to the top. I was getting stronger.

That afternoon I gave in and fed the giant bird that kept showing up and intimidating me into giving him my lunch. I knew it would only encourage more bad behavior, but my heart went out to this hungry creature. I knew what it was to see others eating when you are hungry, as those first days I had a view from my balcony of people eating at the tables on the street in front of the café while I picked tuna out of can and tried to tell myself it was enough. I could certainly spare some food now. I paid it forward and left a few pieces on the ledge, then took my plate inside to finish my meal in peace.

DAY TEN,
OCTOBER 4, 2021

THIS WAS THE DAY I HAD BEEN WAITING FOR. It was the first day I was eligible to take my PCR test again.

I looked at the clock. It was 5 a.m. I was already grappling with huge spiritual questions around both trusting the Universe *and* wanting things to go a certain way. Could they coexist, or did that put me in resistance? I was challenged by surrender and trust. Thy will versus my will, in essence. I did not really have room for negotiation on the outcome of this test. I realized it was a *want*, but it felt like a *need*. I still had some old beliefs tied up inside and connected to a distrust of a separate, judgmental, and punitive deity. I was trying to move forward with my new understanding of spirituality and God as pure unconditional love, and found myself bumping up against some residual pillars from my old framework. It was as if, in the middle of a remodel of my home, I discovered a post inside a wall could not be removed as planned because it was load bearing. I had a whole religious structure built around my faith and relationship with God that was undergoing a remodel, and I had just discovered that a wall I no longer wanted could not be fully removed until we installed new support beams at the foundation. It felt as though I had begun building my complete surrendered trust with the Universe as my new foundational posts, but they were not strong enough just yet to safely tear down the old supports crafted by a fear-based relationship. This mid-construction phase where both posts were in place was extremely uncomfortable. I was labeling things as good or bad, and then reminding myself that it is all *for* me. I wanted to make a plan and was trying to do everything right while knowing there was no wrong way for me to do this and it was okay that it was hard and messy. I was afraid of being punished by having to stay there longer for not trusting and believing enough, that I was being judged for being so afraid. Yet the fear was real, and I couldn't seem to find a way to talk myself out of it. I had not been aware that I had just added my new understandings to my old beliefs, rather than replacing them, and there were contradictions that I had not come face-to-face with until now.

My insides felt like they were tied up in knots, and I could not get out of my head. I reached out to one of my leaders from the AWE program, Kathy, and one of my AWE coaches, Deanne. Deanne responded first, and I told her I needed to talk through some heavy spiritual stuff. She made herself available to me right then and there. I cried at the overwhelming love that her availability to me in this moment signified. I walked her through how I was trying to subdue or release my fear so I would not manifest the very thing I was afraid of, because I know that attention amplifies. But my Fear was stubborn and willful and creating more fear by the minute. To be afraid of my own fear was a new sensation for me, and it was one that ... well ... *scared* me. Deanne invited me to allow the fear to be expressed so it could just move through my body and out. She suggested that perhaps I was holding onto it and trapping it in my body by not allowing it to be expressed. Deanne prayed for me, and I was breathing again. I was gratefully grounded, and we ended our call.

My whole body responded in relief. It was as if Fear was speaking to me: *Yes, see me and understand me and allow me to speak. I just want you to acknowledge me, to care that I am afraid. I will quiet down once seen.* It turns out Fear is like a child, ramping up its volume, throwing a tantrum if needed, just wanting to be seen and hugged and told by an adult that everything will be okay. I needed to parent and comfort my Fear, rather than judge it and send it to its room. I had been responding to Fear the way I had perceived that God responded to me. This was a mirror for me, allowing me to see myself, and God, more clearly. Could I have compassion for all the things I was feeling and experiencing in this moment? Of course I could! *Oh honey, of course you have fear!* I believed that fear and trust must be able to coexist because it felt equally true that I trusted that this was all unfolding in my best interest. I just had certain specific opinions—very strong ones—about what my best interest was at this point. What I kept coming back to was that I was part of the divine Source. I was not just "part" divine, I was one-hundred-percent God-stuff. The whole time I had been there, there had been a battle in my head. I had been afraid to think fearful thoughts for fear of manifesting them, not wanting to cry and despair for fear of putting energy into those outcomes. But of course there was room for the full expression of me. When I said the mantra, *I am safe*, it did not just apply to my physical being. My *thoughts* were also safe. All of them. This was not about exercising mind control, disallowing negative thoughts and fear. Yes, those would likely diminish as I trusted the Universe and my own divinity. And … I was not there yet. And … God would not punish me for being afraid! *I am a yes for God.* Allowing the fullness of my expression gave it an outlet—a release. Feeling the fear and loneliness and despair was the path to letting it go. Pushing it down in denial only made it more insistent, popping up in different places like a game of Whack-a-Mole at the carnival. That was energy misdirection. *Flow, Janine. Let it all flow, up and out. I am in alignment with the divine Source. I am a yes for going home.*

I felt called to the beach to watch the sunrise, so I paused my internal dialogue just long enough to get my toes in the sand on my Warrior Bench. The sun lifted her head over the horizon, emanating an orange glow that invited me into her warmth. Oh yes, I needed this.

I am a poet. It was something I did as a teenager and that I had just returned to in 2020 during the beginning of the pandemic. Since reigniting this creative outlet within myself, I wrote poetry quite often. Sitting on my Warrior Bench, a line I wrote a couple of months ago rose up: *I make peace with You; I make peace with me. Because I am You are We.* This was from a poem about the oneness of humanity, seeing ourselves in each other and beauty in our diversity. I was understanding now that this applied spiritually also. I was wholly divine, and I was not the *whole* divine. There were things I did not see or understand. Micro and macro. I could see the surface of the ocean, and only as far out as the horizon. The detail dissipated the farther away it was on the surface. I could peek under the surface but only in a very small section around me at a time. I think it is also like this with God. I could see, and yet, there was much outside my view. The understandings outside my reach did not negate my core connection with Source. *Because I am You are We.*

I felt centered and strong. This was exactly the morning I needed.

I AM YOU ARE WE

by Janine Valentine

Collectively
We drew
All these ridiculous lines
Between you and me.

Globally
Economically
Anatomically
Philosophically
Ideologically
Methodically
Killing We.
Illogically
Selling the idea
That diversified
Equals adversified

Lamenting our disconnection
While walking the other direction.
Using deflection
As a layer of protection.

Passing judgment,
Critical and repugnant.
If others are our mirrors
We need an adjustment.

Our human dissonance
Can no longer be blamed
On ignorance
Or innocence.

What if we
Could learn to see
The variety
In humanity
As simply
An opportunity
For our chorus
Of beautiful voices
To be harmonies?

I make peace with You.
I make peace with Me.
Each of us
Recognized,
Prioritized,
And I-dentified,
As in
I identify as You.
I identify as We.
As in
There but for the grace of God go I.
As in
I am You are We.

Compassion does not
Require agreement.
Just drop your defenses
And see that
I am You are We.
Join Me.
Let's set ourselves free.

I was reminded of a story in the Bible in which Jacob wrestled with God all night long until the break of dawn. That was what my night and this morning felt like. I wrestled with God. And when it was done, Jacob placed stones in remembrance of the place where God had spoken to him. I wanted a stone in remembrance of this.

I walked down the beach a bit, and then returned to my room to take a shower. I missed being in water. It was hard walking along the water's edge and not being able to go for a swim. The beach was so empty that I probably could get away with it; however, one woman in our travel group had been approached by a police officer upon our arrival on this island when she had on her swimsuit before our boat trip began. He advised her to cover up or he would have to give her a ticket. I was not going to put myself in a situation that had the possibility of adding another complication to this experience. I could have just gone for a swim in my clothing. My mindset at the time was that had I gone for a swim in my clothing, I would not have had a towel. I would have had to sit in the sun to dry off a bit before returning to my room, then shower in my clothes to rinse the saltwater and sand off and find a way to dry them. I had so few pieces of clothing that could be worn for those walks on the beach that the idea of having a whole outfit out of commission for a day or more kept me from swimming in my clothes. I preferred the option of being able to at least get outside whenever I wanted to rather than enjoying a swim and potentially being unable to go for a walk when I next wanted one. Everything felt so limited while I was there. I just accepted many of the limitations without questioning. In hindsight, I regret that I did not allow myself the medicine that floating in that sea would have provided me. It is interesting to me that I could be creative and resourceful in some ways, and so constricted in my thinking in other ways.

The doctor texted me and said he would call me at 11:00 a.m. I felt the shift in my body. I waited with anticipation rather than anxiety.

And then, at 11:00 a.m. when the doctor called, I plummeted back to anxiety as our conversation unfolded. He told me that I must have a negative PCR test to fly into Doha. There were no direct flights to the US from Malé. So the doctor's note stating that I had recovered from COVID-19 and was cleared to fly (which the US would allow for re-entry) won't fly, literally. The doctor now wanted me to wait until Thursday evening (day 13) to test, just to give it the most time possible to become negative. This made sense; there was no point in spending money on an extra test that was too far in advance of my fourteen-day departure window to be used to fly home with. It was just that I had been told by Dr. Usama that I could test at day ten and had assumed that if that test came back negative, I would be able to fly home right away. That was my error. I had not understood that I would not have been able to leave at day ten even with a negative test result. This news meant that the earliest I could fly home would be on day fourteen. I would have results on Friday morning and could fly out on Friday evening as long as the test came back negative. If it came back positive again, I would either have to stay until I tested negative, or perhaps would have to stay another fourteen days. I had gotten conflicting information from the doctor in our various calls. I was not sure he even knew exactly what the protocol was, or that there even was a protocol. Things were changing all the time, and the Maldivian government did not seem to have a well-thought-out or documented plan in place for COVID-positive tourists. I had been reading online that some people continued to test positive for weeks, and even months, after symptoms had stopped. This was not helpful. It just contributed new layers to my fear.

I wondered if I could maybe fly through somewhere other than Doha if I needed to—if Paris or Milan or London might take the doctor's note. I was desperate for a plan B at this point. I needed to believe I would just test negative. I felt good—mostly healthy, probably recovered. *Please, dear God, please, let me test negative on Thursday. I can't get stuck here any longer—physically, mentally, or spiritually. There has been a lot of depth and intensity to this experience. I am worn out.* I became aware that my inside voice was almost chanting a series of *I can't* statements. *I can't get stuck here longer. I can't do this much longer. I can't handle another positive test result. I can't be this isolated any more. I can't take this much longer.* My awareness helped me correct my word choice: *Clearly, Janine, what you meant to say is that you don't* want *to.* Sometimes *I don't want to* can feel like *I can't.* The truth is, I could, and I would if I had to. I was certainly capable. It might suck, and it would be hard and possibly sometimes scary, but I could do much more than I gave myself credit for. I just really did not *want* to have to stay longer, to deal with the fallout, the issues it would create, the hardship, the continued fear and discomfort. But I had already done it, so of course I could do it longer—or deal with the next thing that was not expected or desired. I have been tested and found to be resilient and strong. I trusted myself deeply as a result of those past ten days. My growth spurt was even obvious to myself in this moment.

DAY ELEVEN,
OCTOBER 5, 2021

THE MORNING WAS SUPER STORMY—a bit eerie, somehow.

Tuesday. I kept reminding myself what day it was. The day of the week mattered far less than the countdown to day fourteen, so that was how I thought of the days—by their numbers, one through fourteen. I needed to get through the next two days, and then I could get tested on Thursday, receive my results on Friday morning (which *would* be negative), and fly out Friday evening. That was the only plan I had space for. That was what was going to happen. I needed the win. I had done the work. I had gotten what I was put here to get. The experience was complete. Right?

I messaged Jenny and asked her to go ahead and book my flight out for Friday night. She and I had traveled together before, and I knew her thought process was similar to mine when making travel plans. I trusted her completely to find the right combination of flights and layovers to get me home in a way that was quick, but not so tight that I would worry about missing connections. I did not need any more stress. She said she would book that for me in the morning, since it was nighttime there.

So, how to pass the day? First, another subtitled movie from bed.

The storm passed. It was cooler outside than it had been, cloudy and comfortable. I took a long walk along the beach, just me and the Sea. The waves rushed up gently to kiss my feet. As I walked along the shallow surf's edge, it was not lost on me that although I wanted very much to be home, *here* was profoundly beautiful. I allowed my heart to soar with beauty and gratitude in just that moment, recognizing the duality of loving exactly where I was and simultaneously wanting to be gone from there. I was aware of the beauty of my reality within the present moment. If I allowed my thoughts to slip even one minute to the past or future, the pain of isolation and fear of the unknown would creep in to overshadow the beauty.

I kept an eye out for a stone as I walked—something to take home with me in remembrance of the work I had done there. I almost always brought home sand from beaches I visited, but this time I felt like a rock would be better—something solid I could hold in my hand and reconnect with this journey. As I searched the shoreline debris of rocks and coral and broken shells, I heard a voice in my head—my own thought, except it didn't feel like it originated from me. *Janine, this time it is not about taking something home with you but rather about what you leave here.* Wow. I felt the weight of the truth of this in the same way I felt each footstep on the sand. Imprinted. Supported. Granular.

I unconsciously licked my lips and tasted salt. I *tasted* salt. The Sea was healing me.

I stopped at The Chill Café on my way back to the room and ordered my first coffee since being there. I had so enjoyed my coffee two days ago with the guys from the boat, and I was used to having coffee every morning at home. Now, it felt like a luxury. They presented my coffee to me in the most ador-able little cup, like an espresso. It was thick and smooth, and ... I could taste it! This was *everything.* I took it up to my terrace and enjoyed it very slowly, each sip, the texture, the smell, the flavor. I drank it in, in *all* the ways. In that moment, I felt a perspective shift. I had such long days ahead of me … what if I chose to enjoy every delicious moment? This was a day of my life. Why would I wish it away? I will never get this day back. *Be. With. Where. I. Am.*

My spirits rise and fall with twists and turns like a rollercoaster, I thought. *Yesterday was really hard. Today I have more awareness of beauty. My trust ebbs and flows like the ocean tide.*

DAY TWELVE, OCTOBER 6, 2021

I AWOKE TO THE NEWS that Jenny had booked my flight home for me, for that Friday night. We were moving forward "as if" ... acting "as if" I would test negative on Thursday, "as if" I would fly home on Friday, "as if" I would be home by Saturday evening. It felt unbelievably good to wake up that morning with a ticket for a seat on a series of planes that would take me home. I was leaning hard into this. I ~~needed~~ *wanted* to go home. Playfully, I clicked my bare heels together three times, chanting, "There's no place like home, there's no place like home, there's no place like home."

I envisioned over and over that moment when I would get off the escalator from the train at Denver International Airport and run into my friends' arms. I could see it. I could feel it. This vision was one of the guardrails around my sanity right now.

I went for my walk on the beach with my headphones on this time, blasting music as loud as I could tolerate it. I got lost in the music and literally danced along the edge of the surf. I was delighted by the rhythm of the music mixed with the pulse of the sea, as if it too was dancing along. I felt the sand between and under my toes with each step, and the sun on my face. I twirled with my arms outstretched wide. This was pure joy! I was one with the One. I wondered to myself why I had not thought to do this sooner. I imagined my dance partner, the Sea, was wondering the same thing. We have such a patient Universe.

I walked to the Chill Café, past the same old men who I saw every day sitting at the little tables along the sidewalk, sipping cappuccinos and talking. I ordered tuna kabobs for lunch. I had them one other time and they were amazing and healthy, and I had been craving them ever since. I tried to order them three other times, but they were out. Today, the café had them! I celebrated by adding a slice of coconut cake to my order. My first dessert! I had a flight home in two days; I was feeling a bit more celebratory.

DAY THIRTEEN,
OCTOBER 7, 2021

THIS DAY'S SUNRISE marked my arrival into Thursday, lucky day thir-teen! This was the day I had been waiting for! I could take my PCR test and get the documents needed to be allowed to leave the Maldives the next day. The virus had run its course. The quarantine had run its course. My time here had run its course. I chose to look forward to my clinic visit that afternoon with anticipation of completing my paperwork to clear me to fly out. I told myself over and over that this was not something to fear. I reminded myself that I was healthy. *I shall test negative and return home.* Honestly, though, I had a lot of anxiety simmering under the surface. This was the day I had been both waiting for and dreading because the other side of this coin was not so lucky. The other possible outcome was that I could test positive again. As I unfortunately now knew, lots of people continued to test positive for weeks after symptoms went away, even months. And while most of my symptoms had passed, I was still experiencing some lingering effects of COVID. I could not say for certain that I was no longer contagious because I still felt tired and my senses of taste and smell were sporadic. I could have to quarantine again. The clock could start over.

My old saboteur, restlessness, was trying to rise up. I was a fray of nerves. Understandably. I had both compassion for myself, and certainty that it was unnecessary.

I muscle-tested myself, and my body told me that it was clear of the virus. I believed it for a little while and then slipped back into distrust. It felt a little like a game of tug-of-war; the line went slack and I relaxed for a moment and then some jerk on the other end (*Fear, is that you?*) yanked on the rope and snapped me back into the tension.

I walked up and down the beach and then sat on my Warrior Bench. I asked the Sea if we were done with this colossal time-out yet. *Are you proud of me? Because I am. I am damn proud of myself, for everything I have done and not done and the huge shift in my perspectives and trust levels. I did not curl up in a ball on my bed ... at least not for very long. So I ask again ... can I go home now?*

I sat there very still, just breathing for a few minutes, and then saw myself the way the Sea probably saw me, this tiny person alone on the long stretch of beach, sitting there begging for what I wanted. I apologized to the Universe for acting like a petulant child, screaming and begging for what I wanted over and over again as if the Universe had not heard me or did not care—neither of which was true. I was not going to be punished for being afraid or asking for what I wanted one too many times. Those were old beliefs and ways of being from my childhood rising up. I could hear my parents' frustrated voices telling me to stop asking: "I heard you. You just don't like my answer." "If you ask one more time, you definitely will not get what you want."

I heard religious voices from my past reminding me that God punishes those who do not believe and that the Lord disciplines those He loves. Asking over and over would be seen as lack of faith in God in some circles, inviting divine discipline on ye of little faith. But those voices were not truth—not as I know it now. That old theology I had ascribed to had been about using fear as a motivator. The truth was that I was being heard with patience and compassion, I was seen as who I was and am and will be, one hundred percent known and loved. I was always supported and perhaps even especially so in my moments of fear and distrust. Here was another opportunity for me to see how my old way had been to judge myself for my fear, and my old belief had been that if I was afraid that meant I needed to work more on letting go and fully trusting God. Nope. I *did* fully trust God, and, *of course* I was afraid. Fear did not make trust untrue, and trust could not make fear disappear.

I took more time to just *be* on my Warrior Bench, noticing how my bronze skin glistened with a light coating of sweat from every pore, even on the tops of my shins and backs of my forearms. I ran my fingers lightly along my skin and liked how that felt. The light breeze swirled across my skin, cooling me off a bit. I felt pretty in this moment, and at peace. I saw myself from outside my Self, a glowy bronze woman sitting there on her driftwood log bench by the sea, hair tousled and blowing in the breeze on a Thursday in October, sun-kissed and smiling lightly as she gazed out across the Indian Ocean. Beauty. I, too, was part of all the beauty to be discovered under the fear. There were parts of me that went up in flames here—old beliefs and patterns that were no longer serving me—and as I sat there in the sand sifting through my own sloughed-off ashes, I discovered that I had become even more beautiful. I always was this beautiful; I just had not been able to see it. I had been unearthed.

I looked up at a soft blue, expansive sky that eleven hours from now would be hovering over everyone I loved in Colorado. I sent the sky to them with my love and blessings.

I walked back to the hotel and rinsed my feet at the foot washing station out front before climbing the stairs to my room. I showered and got dressed in the "cleanest" clothes I could. Clean had become extremely relative. I may stink. I was not sure. My sense of smell had only slightly returned and chose random scents to allow into my consciousness. I inhaled deeply on the crotch of my pants and got … nothing. That could not possibly be true. These were the same pants I wore that long first day off the boat and on every trip to the market. I had sweated fear and exhaustion and illness into these pants. Gross. I shrugged and put them on. I had no choice.

It was only 11:00 a.m. Five more hours until I was supposed to go to the clinic. Five hours felt interminable. I did not want to wait. I rationalized with myself that my results would not likely be any different five hours from now. Plus, if I went now, I would be certain to get my results back in time, because last time it took six and a half hours even with the $200 fee I paid to expedite them.

Without much argument with myself, it was decided. I took a taxi to the airport, where there was that second clinic location that the doctor had told me was closer than the one in Malé. It would still be $5 USD each way. I had $15 left, so after my round trip, I would have exactly the $5 cash needed to get back to the airport the next day for my flight out.

It felt weird walking into the airport without any luggage. It also felt like a lifetime ago that I was arriving there with my friends, all giggly and taking selfies. That version of Janine had no idea what awaited her there.

I found the clinic after asking a security guard for assistance. It was to the left of the check-in area. A woman in a burka greeted me, charged my credit card for the PCR test, and then took me in a back room where I pulled my mask down while she took both a throat and a nose culture. She told me she would email me the results tomorrow morning between 6:30 and 7:00 a.m. I wrote down my email address for her and walked back out to the curb where I could get another taxi back to my hotel. It was done. The test was complete. Now I would just wait. *Just*, lol!

The driver of my taxi on the way back to the hotel was Maldivian! He was literally the first Maldivian I had met while there. Everyone had been from Bangladesh or Sri Lanka or India. He was very proud of his country and wanted to show me around. There was another new addition to the island (Hulhumalé being the previous new addition)—a man-made extension of the island. The original island, the side with the city of Malé, was sinking. That was not exactly accurate; the sea levels were rising and would eventually cover the island. The people who lived there were moving to this new higher ground. Resilience in action. The driver told me he would not charge me any extra. He just wanted to show me the new area so when I came back to the Maldives a year later when it was all finished, I could see how it looked completely different. Ha! Sorry, buddy. Absolutely no fault of the Maldives, but at that point I seriously doubted I would ever be returning, and with absolute certainty not the following year.

I did not say this to him, of course. I smiled and thanked him. Yes, it would be lovely to go see this new man-made extension of the island and all the new housing they were creating. It would help pass the time, and I hadn't seen anything other than my little strip of beach and the block of cobblestone street leading to the market the whole time I had been there, other than that one walk to the coffee shop a few blocks away, and the taxi rides from the first clinic and to this clinic, where I had definitely not been in a tourist state of mind. He was a proud tour guide, and I enjoyed his company. We drove over the new bridge and wound our way around an astounding number of high-rise, homogenous apartment buildings. We completed our little drive, and I thanked him. I did wish I had extra money to give him for the kindness and time he gifted me, but I did not. I told him this very honestly, and he graciously accepted my $5 cash payment as I exited the taxi. Blessings on you and your beautiful island and the people there who will fight to save it.

A whole family with three rather loud children had checked into the room next door while I was gone. They were on the terrace, which made me not want to be on the terrace at all. I had no bandwidth left for chaos or noise. I needed quiet. I went into my room and closed the door and the curtains behind me so they would not be staring in at me. I wished I could scream without alarming anyone. The primal release would be helpful.

So now we waited. I had people all over the world waiting with me. I think I may have some PTSD around COVID testing. The last time I had tested and waited, it did not turn out the way I wanted it to. The trauma response to waiting for these results again just two weeks later was real. I was a mess. I kept thinking, *It is out of my hands.* But it was never *in* my hands. This was one-hundred percent surrender. This was raw vulnerability. And it was uncomfortable as fuck.

I could have really gone for a glass of wine. Alas, there was no wine on the island. I had the thought that perhaps I needed to stop vacationing in Islamic countries. I giggled.

I went for another walk on the beach just to move my body in an attempt to quiet my nerves. The beach was crowded with families having picnics because, as I learned from my taxi driver, that day was a Maldivian holiday. There would be a parade somewhere that afternoon. If I knew I was healthy and knew I was leaving the next day, I would probably go enjoy myself at the parade. I was too exhausted from stress to even try. I did, however, enjoy seeing the families on the beach, the women all in burkas, multiple genera-tions gathered together, some playing cards, others talking and laughing. But there was no place for me to relax and linger on my own. All the seating areas were full, and I was self-conscious about my less-than-appropriate clothing. I headed back to my room where the children were still on the terrace play-ing. I smiled and waved at them. I did not want to be the grouchy old lady next door. They had no idea about the stress I was experiencing there in that beautiful place. They were enjoying a holiday, and I was not going to interfere.

I went to bed and slept for a while. I awoke sometime in the middle of the night and journaled more to process the things that were keeping me awake:

O to the M to the G ... is this a "dark night of the Soul"? I am challenged to stay in trust. It rises and falls unpredictably. My body seems to have confidence it is healthy. My heart feels everything is in alignment to go home tomorrow. My soul trusts the Universe's love for me, and that this is all in my highest and best good. It is my damn head causing all this turmoil of swirling what-ifs and fear and distrust. My head wants concrete "for sure" answers, and a plan. I have none.

I slept some more, restlessly, full of terrifying dreams.

DAY FOURTEEN, OCTOBER 8, 2021

MY DAY BEGAN AT 3 A.M. I got only about five hours of sleep total, and given the circumstances, I was grateful for it. I took advantage of being awake while it was still during business operating hours in Colorado and got in about an hour of work. I stopped in time to step out onto my terrace to listen to the 4:40 a.m. call to prayer. I breathed the vibration of the imam's voice deep inside me, capturing this feeling to carry with me that day. This was my own call to prayer, call to expression, call to connection, call to unity, call to compassion. I said another prayer of gratitude for the peace I had found in these calls to prayer that I could invisibly participate in, creating a sense of community and oneness that I so desperately needed. Those men praying that morning had no idea that a fifty-five-year-old American woman was being moved to tears next door, communing with them in love and unity of spirit. This made me smile.

I looked up at the stars. It was a gorgeous, clear night sky, and an amazing number of stars were visible. It had been so stormy since my arrival on that island that this was the first time I got such a clear view of the starry sky from my terrace. I sent this breathtaking patch of sky forward to my loved ones at home, knowing that it would hover over them eleven hours from now. In fact, if all went well, I would fly through this very patch of sky on my way home that night. I relaxed there for a bit, and then immersed myself in the dawning of a glorious sunrise. I took a photo of what hopefully would be my last sunrise there. It was spectacularly beautiful, glowing orange through the trees and reflected on the sea. I felt at peace, filled with so much gratitude and beauty. I decided right then and there that I would print this photo to hang on my wall at home. I wanted to be able to return to this very moment in all the years ahead of me. It felt sacred.

As I walked to the door to go back inside my room, I noticed a dead lizard directly in front of my sliding door. It was honestly amazing that I did not step on it on my way out there in the pre-dawn darkness that morning. Thank God, I did not … I was barefoot. I shivered at the thought. Poor little guy. He was on his back, and the ants were all over him—the same ones that had been in my room feasting on me as well. I wondered if this was a bad or good omen.

I was both fully at peace and also full of anxiety. It was odd. Both were equally true. I knew I was healthy, and it felt obvious that I would get a negative test result, and yet, without that concrete piece of paper in my hands, my mind was simmering in the fears of what if.

And so, I breathed: in five counts, hold five counts, release five counts, hold five counts. Repeat, repeat, repeat. This is called box breathing, and it was helping my nervous system but not my mind. So I headed to the beach for a long walk and another session on my Warrior Bench. I needed to talk this out with God and the Sea. The door downstairs was still locked for the night, but Sahin was asleep behind the front desk and heard me coming down the stairs. He shuffled over, hair all sleep-tousled, and quietly unlocked the door for me to go out. I was so grateful. I could not have gone back upstairs at that point. I needed to be outside. Yes, *needed* it.

I crossed the street and stepped into the sand, taking off my flip-flops and walking through the line of trees. I stopped, momentarily disoriented. My Warrior Bench was missing. After looking both directions along the beach, I finally saw it to the left. My bench was part of a whole seating area now. The Warrior Bench had been presented to me as a gift from the Universe that first day that I was well enough to walk across to this beach. It took my breath away that first morning. It was so perfectly placed in my path. I knew it was mine. I sat there nearly every day, speaking to the Sea and the Universe and my Self. Until this day. It was not mine anymore. I sensed that this was a sign I was going home. This was a sign of confidence and comfort sent to me by my guides. I no longer needed my Warrior Bench. I was leaving. I just needed to stay grounded in this truth while I waited for my PCR test results.

I walked down to the edge of the Sea, and she greeted me, asking, "So, Janine, have you given it some thought? What are you leaving here?"

I pondered for a few minutes and began to list things out loud as I walked in her shallows:

I am leaving here my distrust of, and disrespect for, my body. I listen to my body now in ways I never have. I have tremendous appreciation for all it does for me. I now move my body so it can help me process through my thoughts and emotions rather than shoving them into my joints and organs and bloodstream. I have learned to work alongside my body to heal myself with breath and nature and alignment.

Oh, and I am leaving COVID-19 here, lol!

I am leaving my attachment to outcomes here. I am learning to stay focused on "soon" without attachment to a deadline, being with what is, without needing to know the plan. I can lean into trust in myself and my Source. Things are and will continue to be exactly what, how, and when they are meant to be.

I paused there to acknowledge that there were still some *big* things (like going home that day) that I could move through my body in trust and yet still remain tethered to a particular expectation of outcome. I asked God if that work could be saved for another day. *I have done such deep and challenging work here. Can this be enough for now, please?* I got a sense of peace and took that as God agreeing with me. "Yes, my child," I imagined the Universe whispering, "There is more, and … it is enough for now." I carried with me a new rhythm, a flow, an understanding of myself and the Universe.

I returned to my list of what I would leave on this beach:

The biggest thing I think I shall leave here is my notion of "alone." I so feared being alone, pretty much my entire life. It held me in bad situations more than once because the fear of alone felt worse than the bad situation.

I thought I had not only made peace with being alone but learned to actually savor it the past few years. It turns out that was solitude, which is not the same thing as alone. I began my quarantine experience saying that this was "an alone unlike any other alone. More alone than alone ever was." Now I realized that I was never … am never … alone. I may be physically in solitude, but alone means unsupported, not belonging, unloved. I am one with Source, with those I love (no matter how far away they are physically), and with my community. *I am always supported, always loved. I always belong. I am You are We. Heart to Heart, Womb to Womb. I met Me by the Sea.* My poems literally formed a complete idea. In this moment, I realized for the first time that they were threaded together like a Tibetan prayer flag.

HEART TO HEART, WOMB TO WOMB

by Janine Valentine

Oh honey, I feel your pain,
Your uncertainty, your fears rising again.
I am here
You are not alone.
I shall embrace you
Heart to heart
And womb to womb.

The heart,
Holding sacred space
To love and nourish humanity's shared purpose.
Reflecting outward.
Communal.

I shall meet you there
Our hearts beating against one another
In-sync drumbeats,
Signaling our tribe,
Connecting us to community.
Heart to Heart.

The womb,
Cradling our dreams from conception to birth.
Drawing us inward,
Personal.

I shall hold you here.
Our wombs pressed up against one another.
A deep inner knowing of who we were
Born to be.
Holding that Truth in silent reverie.
Womb to Womb.

Oh, how you are loved!
The Universe conceived you inside its Heart
And prepared you in its Womb.
Open your arms
Stand in your Truth.
I shall embrace you
Heart to Heart
And Womb to Womb.

Four months later while writing this book I would re-read this poem and recognize that my hotel room was like a dark womb for me while I did the necessary growing and receiving, and then my time beside the Sea was my re-birthing process, the Universe embracing me heart to heart, acclimating me to the new world around me before sending me home. The world I would go home to was different because my perspectives had changed, and I had changed. I love it when the poems that came through me reveal new layers of themselves that were meant for a future version of me to discover!

I walked away from my beach on Hulhumalé for the very last time. I was not aware that it would be my last time, as most last times go, so I did not say goodbye. I expected to take one more long walk on that shoreline, consciously soaking it all in with *all* my senses, blessing that beach and the people there and my journey, before heading to the airport that afternoon. So, when I left that morning, I did not even look back over my shoulder at the Sea or my Warrior Bench. I did not carry anything tangible with me from the beach, not a stone or a seashell or a cup of sand. I just turned and walked away, quietly leaving it all there as it was meant to be.

I ordered a coffee and another Maldivian breakfast and came up to my room. It was time. The email from the clinic was to be here between 6:30 and 7:00 a.m., and it was now 7:20 a.m. I logged onto my email, ready to receive my results and move forward into my next chapter.

Nope. No email. But there was a knock on my sliding door. I opened the curtain and saw Sahin standing there. He had come to say goodbye to me because his night shift had ended, and he knew I would be checking out that day. So sweet. He was all smiles and wished me a safe journey and invited me to come back to the Maldives soon. He told me someone would be checking into this room that day and I needed to be out by noon, please. I told him I would, thinking to myself that this meant I would have a long wait at the airport for my 9:00 p.m. flight if I got to go home … but I certainly wouldn't mind, because the wait would mean that I got to go home!

I closed my door as Sahin walked away, and then texted the doctor via WhatsApp, desperate for my results.

Me: Good morning, Dr Usama. I took my test at the airport clinic yesterday about 12:00 p.m. She told me I would receive the results first thing this morning between 6:30 and 7 a.m. I have not received anything yet, and I am understandably quite anxious about it. It has been a long night of waiting. Would you be so kind as to have someone check on them for me? I would really appreciate it.

He did not respond for two long *hours*. I paced and prayed and meditated and paced some more and tried all my tools: box breathing, listening to the love tuner recording, Qi Gong, journaling, listing things I was grateful for, and chanting my mantra, *Be with where you are.* I began to pack because I needed to be out of the room by noon regardless of my results, and keeping my hands busy with an act that symbolized going home was enough to quiet my frantic mind for a few minutes. Finally:

Dr Usama: Good morning. The test came back inconclusive, so I will arrange a test for you again today.

Inconclusive? What did that even mean? I mean, I do know what the word means, but what did it mean that my swabs were inconclusive? Can we count that as negative? Thankfully, the phone rang, and it was the doctor.

"You will need to test again. I need you to go back to the clinic as fast as you can so we can get you retested and get the results back this evening."

I reminded him that I was booked on a flight for which I must check in at 6:00 p.m. I began to cry on the phone and told him that my room had been rented to someone else and that I must check out and bring my luggage to the clinic and use my last $5 cash to get there. When I left this room, I would officially be homeless and out of cash. I needed to be on that flight that night.

"Please," I implored. "Is there anything we can do?"

The doctor suggested that I gargle before I got the throat swab. He would tell the technician as well. He reassured me that he believed it would be all right and asked me how soon I could be at the clinic. I answered that I could be there a little after 10:00 a.m.

"Okay, good," he said. We hung up. He was on my side. We just had to play by the rules, and I understood that.

It was Go Time. The urgency was real. There was no time to stop and think or write or cry or be with myself in this moment. Timing was everything if I wanted to be on that flight that night. I did a quick WhatsApp video call with my sister to tell her what was happening. I was going to lose Wi-Fi when I left my hotel and might not be able to be in touch for a while. I asked her to notify everyone else—my kids, our mom and brother, my closest friends. I promised I would update her as soon as I was able to. Seeing my sister's face via video chat gave me courage and reminded me that I was not alone. She promised to stay up all night if needed. (It was 10:30 p.m. there for her.) She was here with me and for me.

One of the friends my sister notified posted this message in our group thread from the twelve of us who took the vacation together: "Janine's test came back inconclusive. She is getting retested right away and hoping for expedited results so she can catch the 9:00 p.m. flight. She is distraught and will have very limited ability to communicate. Please hold her up in prayer for strength and a negative result." I wouldn't see this message until after I got home, but the word distraught struck me. The definition of distraught is "deeply upset and agitated; frantic, deranged." Yep. That summed it up well. I was distraught.

I finished packing very quickly—so quickly that I would later realize I had left my razor and shampoo in the shower, and I had put several things into the bag I would be checking that I would normally want in my carry-on backpack for the flight home. But no matter. I could go without things. I had certainly proven that in the past two weeks. Comfort was not priority. Getting home was all that mattered.

I carried my own luggage downstairs since my phone still did not work and it really did not make sense to go down without it and then send someone up to get it for me—although that made almost as much sense as ordering room service that way. I did have to pause a couple of times on my way down. I had not yet regained all my strength. I asked Rubel to call a taxi for me and then rather quickly said goodbye to him as the taxi pulled up to the curb almost immediately. I did not feel like I had time to look around for the last time, to take it in, to exhale gratitude for this place and the people. Then again, I was not doing much exhaling. I am certain I was forgetting to breathe during much of my exit process.

I rode to the airport in silence. I felt terrified, and containing that was taking everything. I had gone deep inside myself. I handed my very last $5 to the driver and walked like a zombie into the terminal and directly to the clinic I visited yesterday, only this time with luggage.

A young woman in yet another black burka greeted me inside the small clinic. I told her my name. She was expecting me. The doctor had spoken to her already, and she directed me to a sink in the back where I could gargle. I had a bottle of water with me, thankfully. It was 10:15 a.m., so I paid another expedite fee on my credit card so I could get these results in three or four hours rather than the usual eight to twelve hours, since check-in for the flight I intended to be on was at 6:00 p.m. The airlines were very strict with their check-in times there. That was not a suggested time; it was the assigned time. An airport employee stood at the front of the check-in line and asked to see your ticket. You could not get in line before that scheduled time, and when they closed the check-in window for your flight, that was it. You either made it or missed it. I did the math. I should know by 2:30 p.m. She took me to the cubicle area where I tested yesterday and motioned for me to take down my mask. She swabbed my throat and then my nose. I surprised myself when I suddenly wondered if I could pay her to take the swabs for me, to buy the result I wanted. People probably do that somewhere, right? There was probably a black market for fake test results even. The thought did not linger and was not something I would ever have done because it was not even remotely who I am. I am such a rule-follower that my friends sometimes make fun of me for it. And if I were going to start breaking rules, this was not the place to do it. Breaking the law there, where my rights as an American citizen were void, could have been catastrophic—an international incident, even. It was, however, a clear indicator of how desperate I felt. In that very moment, I had developed a communal compassion for those who *do* make those types of choices out of desperation. Survival instinct is real, and it may not align with our sense of right and wrong.

I walked out of the clinic, luggage in tow, thinking, "*This is all I have. I carry it with me. I live here now, at the airport, until I can test negative.*" It was not rational, of course. There were ATMs at the airport, so I would be able to get more cash with my credit card … *finally*! I debated whether I should do that now, proactively, or if that might only manifest a longer stay. I could wait and just do it when and if I needed it. But would I be of sound enough mind to handle that task if I got another positive test? I was not sure, honestly. I was having a full conversation in my head, Fear and Reason disagreeing as usual.

I found a sign with the airport Wi-Fi password and set it up on my phone. I moved to the very edge of the open-air terminal and sat down at a table. There was no wall or window in front of me, only the road that brought me there with taxis lined up on the curb, and the sea on the other side of that. It was a gorgeous view. *This will help calm me.*

Instead, it opened me up. As usual, the Sea pulled down my defenses; the very sight of her took away my walls and stripped me bare right there in front of everyone in this airport. In an instant I felt all the vulnerability and raw emotion inside me rising like a tsunami. I began to cry. Hard. I no longer had any control … but then, I never really did anyway. I no longer had the *illusion* of any control. I struggled to breathe. I felt dizzy. I was both grateful for the mask, which hid the contortions of my face, as well as my tears to some extent, and also resentful of the way it constricted the flow of fresh air my lungs and body needed. I wanted to get out of there, but where? I began walking outside the airport, and I lost vision in my left eye.

I messaged my sister to tell her the test was complete, and I had four hours to wait, and I couldn't breathe, and I couldn't see out of my left eye, and I was losing my shit right in the middle of the airport with strangers walking past me. She texted back to inform me that I was likely having a panic attack. Fuck.

"Do your box breathing," she suggested.

And that was the last text that got through before I lost my Wi-Fi connection. Just as well. I could not keep typing, and I had nothing else to say. I needed to keep walking. I would walk the fear away, because that was a thing now, right? I took some deep breaths and held, released, and held. The breathing and the movement were stabilizing me a bit.

Practical Me spotted an ATM machine. So, there *was* still a part of me that was functioning and would help me survive whatever was next for me. That was comforting to discover. I decided (hoped) that cash might empower me. It could at least provide me with options during these next four hours, and if needed, beyond. It had not been possible for me to get to a bank these past two weeks, so I felt like I should take advantage of the opportunity to make my next two weeks there a bit more comfortable if they were deemed necessary. I would need cash just to get to another hotel for the night. *I am not calling this in, mind you. I am being proactive, and I am happy to just take this cash on home with me, thank you very much, Universe.*

I got in line behind a man already at the ATM and stood the appropriate midpandemic distance behind him. He finished up, and before I could step forward, in swooped another man. He just stepped in front of me without even looking at me. He had not been in line. I was not sure where he came from. It was as though he had just been walking by and did not see me and stepped right up to the ATM machine. Okay … well, it was not like I was in a hurry. I decided it did not matter, and I waited for him to finish. And then—I kid you not—it literally happened again. Another man just stepped right in front of me. I was already stepping toward the machine, and he just sidestepped me.

Unbelievable! Yet, actually, it was quite believable. Women truly were considered "less than" men in this culture, and the superiority of the masculine was just a given. It probably had not occurred to either of these men that I, a woman, was waiting to pull money from an ATM. Women were taught to be submissive here. We were expected to step aside and let men pass. I knew this from experience over the past couple of weeks. Since this was not how I was raised as a female in my culture, I had no idea I was meant to step aside if a man approached from either direction. As a result, I nearly got stepped on several times on the sidewalk in front of my hotel on my way to and from the beach by men who acted as though I were invisible. They literally had no intention of moving around me. It seemed a subconscious thing, like it never crossed their minds that we might not move out of their way.

There were similar expectations of women in my American culture as well; they were just less blatant. As a woman, I was far more aware of potentially being in someone's way than men were and had certainly experienced men moving through store aisles and down sidewalks with a perceived expectation that women would move out of their paths—because we always did. There were also men in America who were more conscious of sharing space and made room for women to pass. We would call this chivalrous, which feels a bit generous for what should perhaps just be labeled as human kindness. As a woman, I felt deeply offended each time it happened. I resented being treated as though I and my sister-women were inconsequential. Not being seen ... this was another type of discrimination and victimization. We have all done this at some point. I know there have been times when I refused to acknowledge the presence of men experiencing homelessness, mostly out of my own fears and discomfort. But standing in front of the ATM machine, waiting on yet another man who had diminished me, as an American woman used to a certain level of freedom and rights, I felt pissed off. My rights had been violated. Except my rights did not travel with me from America to the Maldives. I thought of them as mine, a part of me, something I carried with me in my physical being. Not true. Whatever rights we had were bestowed on us by our governments and our cultures, and there were physical borders that contained them. Step outside those borders and our rights remained behind. We may all need to remind ourselves of this as we travel to other countries and cultures around the world. We may disagree with some of the things we encounter, but we are guests in another's home. In my current emotional state, however, being unseen and having my needs disregarded felt unbearable. These two men were just two representatives of all the perceived barriers between me and my cash, between me and my home, between me and my comfort. I knew it was not wise to confront this man or even mumble a grievance aloud to myself, so I quietly walked away. I did not know where I was going. I just needed to walk, and I needed away.

I saw a sign for HIH, a hotel that offered a day pass for its pool. I knew this because back on the boat I had suggested that our group find a hotel near the airport that had a pool that might offer a day pass, since we had nearly ten hours between leaving the boat and checking in at the airport. A couple of the ladies got online and found this place, and that was where the ten of them went while Wendy and I went to the clinic for me to retest and then waited in the "holding cell" all day. They were all at the pool at HIH, hoping I would get a negative result and we would join them for a bit before the flight. I recognized the name of the hotel and knew a day pass there would provide reliable Wi-Fi so I could be in touch with my friends and family, a pool so I could cool off and calm down, and a place to store my luggage for the long wait ahead. I remembered there was a free shuttle to HIH, but it seemed I had likely passed where that would logically be, and I also remembered that the website said it was only an eight-minute walk from the airport. Obviously, I had already begun the walk, so I guessed this was what my body or my guardian angels had decided we were doing next. I knew the hotel would take my credit card, so my mind quickly got on board with the new plan.

The walk, however, was not pedestrian friendly. The sidewalk was broken and jagged and then abruptly ended. I was now walking in the street, which was rough cobblestone with sand all over it. Mind you, I was dragging my suitcase behind me, wearing a heavy backpack with my laptop in it, dressed in clothing that covered me as appropriately as possible, which was making me even hotter, and wearing a face mask. It was a lot of work, and I had not recovered my energy fully. This was the most I had exerted myself in two weeks, and it was also in the middle of the hottest part of the day. My wheeled bag kept getting stuck on the sandy cobblestone cracks. I would lift it and start again, then get jolted as though I were a dog on a leash that had gotten too far in front of my owner. Sometimes my suitcase would actually flip over onto its side as if protesting the rugged terrain. The wheels were getting trashed, but I could not carry it, and I was far enough into the walk that I was now committed to arriving. Turning around would be just as much effort with no pool to welcome me in that direction.

I persevered. I was sweating profusely. Even the bridge of my nose was emitting its own sweat. I could see the hotel, but from the angle of my approach I was uncertain whether I could get access directly to the hotel from this road. I began to be concerned that I may have to go all the way around to get in. A police officer walking toward me on the road asked in broken English if I needed help. Ha! Understatement of the year. Clearly, not many tourists chose to walk to this hotel. Or perhaps they simply did not usually look as pitiful and bedraggled as I must have. Inside my mind, I briefly envisioned a response where I burst into tears and said that, *yes,* I needed help please, and flopped onto the ground in a heap. I wanted a bottle of water and a shower and someone who could figure all this out for me while I took a nap in an air-conditioned room, please. In real life, I smiled and pointed to the hotel and asked if this road would get me there. He nodded and walked on past me. I carried on.

I arrived in such a state that the bellman took both of my bags and rushed me over to a chair to sit down, insisting that he would bring everything to me to check me in. Clearly, I looked as precariously not okay as I felt: tear- and sweat-streaked, bright red face, overheated, frizzy hair from the humidity, beat-up and sandy luggage in tow, breathing hard, dusty, just freshly out of a panic attack. I gratefully accepted a seat in the gorgeous lobby, which was fully air-conditioned. I felt like a homeless woman who had been allowed to rest for a moment in this luxury hotel. Then I laughed to myself (possibly making me look like a mentally unstable homeless woman) because, in fact, I *was* a homeless woman at the moment, and this was *exactly* what was happening. This was a resort hotel, the kind of place I was not able stay at during my quarantine because they would not have allowed me to check in without a negative COVID test. They did not ask for proof of my PCR test for the day pass, probably because a day pass meant I was flying out, and I obviously had to have that to do so. I paid $67 on my credit card for a day pass and went into the restroom to change into a swimsuit. I confirmed in the mirror that I did indeed look as bad as I had imagined. I was frankly a little surprised that they did not call an ambulance. They may have discussed it among themselves. I checked my bags in with the bellman after changing, and he pointed me down a hallway to the pool area.

This was how the tourists were enjoying this island and it was *very* different from how I had been living. And I did not even have a single dollar on me to tip this bellman, my new hero. Oh so grateful, and oh so humbled. I had never experienced the parallel emotions of something being such an eager, grateful "yes" crying out inside me, alongside such a hard, tearing away of my ego, in order to receive this gift.

The pool was gorgeous. The water was so inviting. I could not wait to get in and cool off and rinse away the sweat and fear of the day. To float, to relax, to breathe. But first, I set up on a lounge chair under the palm trees at the far end, where I could look at the pool when I sat up, and look at the sea when on my stomach. I could see the airport where I had just come from. I got on the Wi-Fi and connected with my sister and two best friends, Lois and Wendy, who were all still up with me even though it was the middle of the night for them. They were in this with me in the only way they could be, keeping the proverbial light on as long as I remained in the darkness of the unknown. They had each vowed to be available to talk at any time. They were going to stay awake until they knew I was safely on that plane that night, or worst case, settled into my next hotel. This was love, holding the high watch for each other. I felt partnered, like I had resources at the ready if any new problems or questions arose—a whole team, clear-headed and motivated, ready to figure it out with me. They couldn't be there with me, but they were showing up. My soul sisters. I let them know where I was and that I was okay. They encouraged me to use the water to calm myself, to get back into my body, to find trust again. They spoke wisdom into my dark and dusty mind, which felt like the aftermath of a tornado.

Almost on autopilot, I put my phone away and climbed down the ladder into the pool, immersing myself step by step into the most refreshing and clean water I had felt in over a month. I swam a couple of leisurely laps to get my whole body moving and gliding, until I found my own fluidity and was able to feel the water on my skin, which had apparently gone numb at some point in my journey there. I floated. I soaked. I normalized my body temperature and stabilized my emotions. I allowed Fear and Hope and Trust space to coexist within me. I asked them to hold hands and have compassion for one another through the rest of this process. Getting in water worked every time.

It was now 3:00 p.m., thirty minutes beyond the time frame that my results were expected, yet no news. I could not stand it. I was worried that the technician wrote down my email incorrectly. I could not enjoy this place any longer, not that *enjoy* was the right word for what I had been doing anyway. All I was doing was watching the clock move interminably slowly. I decided I just needed to be at the airport clinic, waiting for my results there. It was not as comfortable as this, but it was in the real world of what was happening right now, and this hotel was not. I could not pretend this was reality. I got what I needed from being here, I was grateful for the oasis in my desert, and now it was time to continue my journey.

I changed back into my uncomfortably still wet-with-sweat travel clothes and retrieved my bags from the bellman. This time, I took the free shuttle back to the airport. I felt shame that I could not tip the bellman on the way out, nor my driver upon arrival back at the airport. It was what it was. I thanked them both from my heart and let it go.

The clinic did not yet have my results. I had not missed an email. The technician graciously offered to let me wait in the back waiting room. No one else was in there, and this part of the clinic did not seem to be in use. She gave me a water bottle, and I took off my shoes and reclined on a couch. It was cooler in there than in the open-air airport just outside the door, and this couch was far more comfortable than the airport attached-row plastic chairs. I waited. I prayed. I waited. I pleaded. I waited. I cried. I waited. I breathed. I waited.

At 5:30 p.m., my friend Kelly Grace messaged me on WhatsApp: "That's your plane. Your seat." She was envisioning me on that plane, claiming it for me as mine, and I believed her. It was extremely comforting and became my mantra for the next half hour. And then, just before 6:00 p.m., the technician arrived carrying a piece of paper.

"Your results, they are in," she said, handing me the paper. She pointed to "NOT DETECTED" and smiled. "Negative!" she exclaimed.

I wanted to hug her, but we were in a COVID clinic and that was not appropriate. I looked her in the eyes and said, "Oh thank God! Thank you, thank you, thank you!!!" I was tearing up for what must have been the hundredth time that day, but those tears were of release and gratitude. Relief rushed through my whole body like a giant seventh wave. I was going home! HOME!

I texted *everyone*. It was 6:00 a.m. at home, so most people were awake or would be soon. "It is negative! I am coming home! Oh my god, oh my god, oh my god!" Word spread across the world like wildfire.

I texted my mom and sister, "It's negative!!!! I'm coming home!!!"

They responded in a series of short bursts. "Oh babe. Oh hallelujah!!!!!!!!!!!!!! You're coming HOME!!!!!!!! You did it. OMG I'm so proud of you. I'm sosososososo happy!!!!!! A huge AMEN—celebrating with everyone!!"

I waited thirty hours from when I had my first test at noon the day before until I got my final results that day at 6:00 p.m. Thirty hours! It was like knowing there had been fifty-two stairs to my room. The number did not actually surprise me, and yet it felt *big*.

I quickly completed my health form online that was required to leave the Maldives. I could not complete it until I had my negative PCR test result to upload, so this was not something I could have done while I was waiting. It took four attempts on the spotty airport Wi-Fi, but I did not mind. I was going home. I completed the form just minutes before 6:00 p.m. and a voice over the loudspeaker was literally calling my flight number for check-in right as my phone screen flashed the QR code indicating my form had been accepted. This was what I needed to scan in order to check in. Perfect timing. I picked up my bags and walked into the security line to officially begin my journey home.

I got through the first security line, went straight into another line to check my bag, and got my seat assignments and boarding passes. I did not even care at all where I was sitting. Honestly, I would have stood in the aisle all the way home without complaining once because … I was going *home*!

Standing in line, I texted a friend, "I know it probably sounds weird and certainly irrational, but there was a part of me that lost hope … that really started to think I might never get home."

She responded, "We would have gotten you home no matter what. Even if we had to fly back there and kidnap you."

That had crossed my mind too, lol! My friends were just as crazy as I was.

Yet another security line, and then I was in a food court area. Food. I had not eaten at all that day. I used my credit card to buy a wrap sandwich and a bottle of water. I sat at a *table*, next to other tables with people, and ate my meal. I had not eaten a meal at a table, or around other people, in weeks. These were all strangers, yet I felt part of a community. The healed leper was returning to society, unceremoniously. After a leisurely casual but emotionally significant dinner, I moved to the gate to board my first flight at 9:00 p.m. Four hours to Doha, Qatar.

DAY FIFTEEN,
OCTOBER 9, 2021

WE LANDED IN DOHA, and I had a somewhat tight transfer. All the passengers went through security as we exited the plane, and then I walked all the way to the other side of the airport, which thankfully was fairly empty since it was the middle of the night. I quickly popped into the restroom (and messaged my sister from the bathroom stall because I was so excited that there was toilet paper), and then maneuvered through security a second time to get to the next gate. I got there right as it was time to board, walking straight out of security and onto the plane. Perfection. This would be the longest of three legs. The flight time was just over fifteen hours. To my delight, I got a window seat. I had hopes of leaning against it and getting some sleep. I have a history of being unable to sleep on planes. I was even more delighted when we started pulling away from the gate and it was confirmed that there was no one in the middle seat next to me. I truly had not cared where I was sitting, and that was still true, and also … this felt like such a gift to me from the Universe. Going home was enough; the window seat and empty middle chair were lavish extras.

The next fifteen hours were hazy. I felt relief. The adrenaline was leaving my body. I dozed on and off and watched movie after movie—without subtitles! The time passed surprisingly quickly. I imagined being home, seeing my friends and family, the hugs, my reunion with my dogs, being inside my apartment, sleeping in my bed.

We landed in Chicago, and the flight attendant said over the intercom, in English, "Welcome to the United States of America!" A physical surge of gratitude and relief and happiness rose up in a giant bubble and burst forth from my body in sudden tears, and an audible moan. I wondered if the guy sitting in the aisle seat of my row thought perhaps I was extra patriotic. This made me smile even more. My mask hid the odd contortions my face was making as it smile-cried. I was back in my country. I was nearly home. I could drive home from there if anything were to go wrong at this point. I had made it. Nothing would stop me from getting all the way home now.

I deplaned and went to baggage claim to pick up my checked suitcase so I could go through US customs with it. The man behind the glass in customs asked me how long I was in the Maldives. I had to do some quick math because all I had been absorbed with over the past two weeks was the countdown of the fourteen days of quarantine.

"Twenty-six days," I responded. Twenty-six days … dang. His eyes widened, and he asked me what I was doing for that length of time. I could not bring myself to confess to him that I had been recovering from COVID-19 in a mandatory two-week quarantine for half of that time, because I did not want to raise any red flags when I was this close to home. I smiled and told him I was snorkeling and enjoying the sea, which was true—for the first half of my experience. He nodded and handed my passport back to me.

As I pondered that number, twenty-six days, I recalled that during a weekend intensive with my coaching group on the Sunday just before I left on my vacation, we each drew a card from a self-care deck. We were to commit to practicing whatever we drew for the next thirty days. What is so crazy is that I drew a card that read "Time Alone." I was gone twenty-six days, and I drew the card four days before flying out. Thirty days exactly. Foreshadowing at its best. And the Universe laughed, "Bwa-ha-ha!"

I rechecked my suitcase and ceremoniously turned my phone off airplane mode for the first time since boarding the airplane in Denver a month ago. I could now make and receive phone calls and texts without using WhatsApp. I was reconnected. Elation!

First stop in the terminal: Starbucks. I ordered an iced green tea, and it had become autumn while I was gone so pumpkin bread was now on the menu. I embraced the new season and added a slice to my order. I chatted on the phone with a few friends while I waited to board my final flight. This leg would be just two and a half hours to Denver. Easy peasy.

Upon landing, I texted my friend Jenny to let her know we were wheels down on the tarmac in Denver. *Squeee!* She said she was parked in the waiting area at the airport and instructed me to text her again from baggage claim so she could time meeting me at the curb. This was our normal protocol for picking up friends at the airport. I didn't question the plan, but I can admit to a little private disappointment that my arrival would be so *normal*; nothing about my homecoming felt normal. No matter. I was *home!* I deplaned and walked down the same long hallway I had walked up with my friends when we were leaving Denver together a month before. I passed the wine bar where we had a drink together as we filled out paperwork and waited to board, full of excitement and anticipation. I felt a wave of light-headedness wash over me, and my abdomen tightened. It felt a bit like I was a ghost from the future, invisibly visiting the scene of a crime that we had not yet known was going to happen. I reminded myself that I likely had a little PTSD as I remembered sitting there twenty-six days ago, laughing with my friends and sipping wine, unaware of what was going to happen. I guess that is how it always is, right? There is the before and the after. Trauma separates time and creates a different perspective.

I got on the train to the terminal where the luggage would arrive. I went up the escalator after getting off the train and made the turn to head to baggage claim. And there, right there in front of me, was my whole beautiful tribe. They were holding balloons and flowers and teddy bears and a giant sign that read, "Welcome Home Janine – Queen of doing hard things – We ♥ you!"

In my head, I ran to them. But in reality, I was exhausted, and it almost felt like a mirage. They were my water in the desert. I walked in my dream fog state over to them and collapsed into their arms. Now it was real. All of us were crying and laughing and applauding and just holding onto one another for a very, very long time. Human touch. Oh my, you do not notice how much you need it until you are deprived of it. I had not even shaken anyone's hand or so much as accidentally touched anyone in two weeks. People go much longer than this deprived of human touch, I realize. That should never happen. We need each other. Being loved like this ... it is beyond words. *I am blessed. I am grateful. I am HOME.*

We moved en masse to get my suitcase. One of my friends, Julie, upon seeing my small suitcase as it came off the carousel, exclaimed, "That's it?!" Ha! Yes, girl, that's it. That was just one of my many challenges. I had always been proud of my ability to pack light. That may be past tense now, though. I think I might be packing steamer trunks from here on out!

Only Jenny and Julie would be driving me home. They had all come from different directions to meet there. I was not ready to go our separate ways. I wanted to lie down in a pile on the airport floor with these women, close enough to feel their skin and hear their breathing, to hold onto them tightly and just cry together in relief. Instead, I suggested we walk to a bar in the airport and order a bottle of champagne. They unanimously agreed, and we formed a parade of sorts, with our signs and balloons and flowers, marching to the hotel bar attached to the airport. We toasted my homecoming and shared stories from all sides. I finally had the bandwidth to ask them about their experience of leaving me there. I knew that had to have been ridiculously hard, and yet while I was there I just did not have the capacity to hear what that was like for them. I had no space for more sadness. Now, with my feet on American soil, I wanted to hear their stories.

They shared that they were all traumatized by it, and that the trip home was a solemn and quiet one. No loud conversations or raucous laughter. They did not regale one another with glorious stories from our vacation. They were all sort of inside themselves and dazed. They felt the absence of me, a heavy emptiness that traveled all the way home with them. They were heartbroken and had to deal with their own grief and guilt and helplessness about the situation. They had the added fear of testing positive themselves once they got home, so they all took more COVID tests over the course of that first week, half expecting that several more of them would end up infected since we had all spent time together on the boat. None of them got it. There was a collective sigh of relief when they passed the window of exposure. Then, they all turned their attention to preparing for my return, and welcoming me home. And there we were. We were together. We were in it together all along. I was not alone. I never was.

There was more.

I arrived home, and as I walked up the stairs to my apartment, I saw that my front entry had been decorated with shiny streamers and giant balloons by two of the ladies who went on the trip with us who had not been able to meet me at the airport.

I stepped inside the front door to find my apartment filled with rose gold and white balloons and colorful ribbons everywhere. There were more flowers and several gift baskets filled with champagne, bath salts, candles, and chocolate on my kitchen island and dining room table. There was the softest blanket ever and a huge bowl of fruit. And worth its own mention … *two* Costco-sized packages of toilet paper! I opened my fridge, and it was *full* … so full that my friends had obviously needed to rearrange my shelving to get everything to fit! It was fully stocked with fresh vegetables, salmon, salads, hummus, and so much more. I felt incredibly cared for. I went from a small room with very scarce resources just two days before to this incredible abundance. What an overwhelming contrast.

I couldn't wait any longer for my reunion with my fur babies. I opened the door to my bedroom, where they were patiently waiting for me. I fell to the floor in a big puppy pile, with them gleefully pouncing around me and licking my face. They were very happy to see me, and also, I could tell they had been very well cared-for because they weren't frantic. When they've been scared by something or left alone for too long, they whimper as they try to get as close to me as they possibly can. That was not the case, even after my being gone nearly a month. This was so reassuring to me. Everything was okay. We all survived.

RE-ENTRY

THAT FIRST NIGHT HOME, I cuddled in my bed under a big, fluffy comforter. I had also brought the new super soft blanket and teddy bear from my friends into bed with me. I wanted to keep touching them, along with my dogs snuggled up next to me. It was a softness binge. I had not realized I had missed "soft" until I was in that bed. I was *so* hungry for the texture of soft. In the Maldives, I had only a sheet on my bed and scratchy towels and hard tile floors without rugs. I had not named it while I was there, but it was a deprivation of softness ... in all ways. I buried myself in this puddle of softness and bliss and went to sleep feeling *safe* for the first time in fifteen days.

I awoke at 2:00 a.m. due to jet lag. I was hungry, and I knew I could actually do something about it this time. I walked to the kitchen, hyperaware of every footstep, feeling the softness of the carpet under my bare feet. I opened my silverware drawer and a guttural sob lurched up from deep inside my core and escaped my throat. I leaned forward over my kitchen island and just wept over the abundance of silverware at my fingertips, the *ease* of resources. I was struck by all I had taken for granted until I experienced its lack. For the past two weeks, almost everything had been hard. Now, I just opened a drawer and there was everything I could ever want. It felt decadent. A part of me was ashamed that I never realized what a privilege it was to have that drawer full of utensils, many of which I used only a couple of times a year. I have traveled to poverty-stricken areas. I have witnessed the lack in many communities, and there was a difference between seeing it and living it. Probably, the things I went without would not have seemed like such a big deal to me if I had not also been sick, quarantined, and isolated from my friends and resources in ways that meant I was not really able to change my circumstances or get things I needed or wanted. This magnified the lack.

I heated up some food in my microwave. Wow! Warm food, ready in seconds. It felt *so* good in my mouth and my belly.

I went back to bed for a couple of hours, mostly just lying there snuggling the dogs and dozing. I got up at dawn and made coffee. *I made coffee.* The independence of this! I took my mug onto my balcony with a blanket and sat there quietly watching the sunrise. I received the sky that I knew was over my hotel in the Maldives just eleven hours before … a sky that I missed while I was traveling home. And then I saw it—the overlay. It was magical. The view from my balcony was nearly identical to the view from my terrace in the Maldives. I saw glimpses of the water through the trees right below the sunrise … it was a pool and pine trees here, rather than the ocean and willowy trees there, but the same placement. I now had a walking path instead of a cobblestone road, but it wandered beneath my balcony in the same direction. There was a recreational area just off to the left in both places. Here at home it was a putting green for golf, and on the island it had been a rack of paddleboards and canoes for use on the beach. I had not been able to see the familiarity when I was in quarantine, but it took my breath away now.

The air here had changed. It was cool and autumnal. The leaves had shifted from greens to vivid oranges, yellows, and reds. There were pumpkins and scarecrows on peoples' porches. I left here in the summer and returned in the fall. As I watched some of the leaves float gently to the ground, I became aware that the trees were reflecting back to me—acknowledgment of all that I had released in the past couple of weeks. Together, we were letting go and moving into the next season. I was ready. I embraced the shift of the seasons. It felt appropriate, nature meeting me exactly where I was internally.

Everyone wanted to talk to me and connect and hear my story. Of course they did! I was grateful to have so many people in my life who love and care for me and were making the effort to reconnect and welcome me home and share in my stories and love on me and take care of me. I just did not feel like talking yet. It was exhausting to try to synopsize the experience into sound bites. This was a deeply personal and spiritual experience. I was clear that it was meant to be shared. I knew I would write about it—in this very book. I just needed time to find words, to honor myself and my experience, to collect the fullness of what happened on the other side of the world in two short, yet very long, weeks.

"How are you?" This was the question everyone asked me for days and weeks after I got home. I struggled with this question more than any other. *How am I? Hmmm. Filled with gratitude. Exhausted. Jet-lagged. Traumatized. Profoundly changed. Internal. Home.*

I am a warrior.
I am capable.
I am vulnerable.
I am community.
I am loved.
I am supported.
I am resilient.

I did not choose to face my fear. It was not a choice. It just rose up and swallowed me. In that dark, cavernous stomach, I used my tools to light a match. And I kept that flame going. I lit my path home. I did hard things. I was brave. I was scared. Both things are true.

ASSIMILATION

IN THE WEEKS AND MONTHS THAT FOLLOWED, I sometimes felt like I did not fit into my old life anymore. The changes inside me were that profound. It felt like an identity crisis. I found myself unable to plan ahead or even keep track of my schedule beyond whatever that day held. I wasn't nearly as concerned about how things turned out or what was happening around me in the world as I used to be. I found myself shrugging it off, assuming it was exactly as it was meant to be. Nothing bothered me because it all paled in comparison to being home.

I had awakened to truths that changed the way I would move forward. I was considering how I ate only healthy foods during my quarantine, even after my symptoms subsided. I never once overate in a stress response while I was there, and I splurged on something with sugar in it only one time. I moved my body physically when I felt overwhelmed with emotions or stress. I got outside, skin in the sun and toes in the sand, when I felt disconnected. I was listening to my body and my intuition. It was interesting that I was capable of making healthy decisions for myself when my life literally depended on it. Yet, it wasn't until I got home that it occurred to me that my life *always* depended on what I did or did not do, the changes I made or didn't make, the fears I faced or didn't face. The quality and longevity of my life depends on my choices and actions (or inaction). Why does the "your life depends on this" motivation work only when we are in fear of possible imminent consequences? As I moved back into my life at home, I vowed to maintain my physical, emotional, and spiritual wellness as my highest and first priority. My rhythms had changed. I was more tuned in to what I needed, moment by moment, and willing to act on that, whereas in the past I would have "pushed through" or delayed it or numbed it out for the sake of productivity or convenience.

I had a lot of physical symptoms for months after getting home. I was unsure if these were left over from COVID, or from traveling, or even from the prolonged stress. Probably all three were involved in some way. I got a referral to a Reiki practitioner from my dear friend Laura, and I booked an appointment in the hopes that the practitioner could help me identify what was going on inside me physically and spiritually. At our first meeting, I shared my recent experience with her and described my ongoing symptoms, which included frequent headaches, occasional dizziness, ringing in my ears off and on, one eye twitching that was driving me crazy, trouble with my short-term memory (I felt like I couldn't retain information like I used to), and disrupted sleep (and I used to be a really good sleeper). I felt like I cried more often and tears just showed up sometimes. I had intestinal issues, lower back pain, and a spot between my shoulder blades that itched all the time.

She looked me in the eye and told me these were *all* classic ascension symptoms. I had no idea what she meant. She explained it to me, and honestly, it still did not make much sense. Over the next few weeks, I researched it on my own and realized it was exactly what I was experiencing. It has been astounding to me how often my spiritual awakening happens prior to my understanding of it. It gets ahead of me, and then I play catch-up, learning the language needed to describe and interact with it. As I educated myself about these ascension symptoms in order to understand and hopefully heal my symptoms, I learned that many of these symptoms were related to having suppressed my emotions and my true self for many years. It occurred to me that to make ourselves smaller requires compression. It makes so much sense now, but I had never considered where I had gone for all those years when I had been trying to be what everyone expected me to be. We are energy beings. The energy that was Janine was still inside my physical body, and my body had devised ways to hold it all in for me, to keep me safe as I perceived the world seeing my true self as danger. I was now releasing that constriction and allowing myself access to express myself, therefore quickly shedding the trapped emotions and trauma from inside my physical body, causing physical symptoms. The worst of these were severe abdominal cramps that came on without warning and sometimes lasted for a week or more. The pain was so bad that it caused me to vomit with each spike. I had all kinds of bloodwork and tests and ultrasounds, and they all came back healthy and normal. I came to understand that my beloved body was actually purging itself all at once of toxic beliefs, suppressed emotions, trauma memories, and built-up stress. What I originally thought of as symptoms were actually signs that my body was healing itself and taking me to the next level. I have misunderstood myself for such a long time. My regard for my physical body has never been higher.

During my meditation one day, a phrase rose up inside me. *My body is a conduit, not a container or a vessel. A conduit.* Because of my experience in the Maldives, I now had a new understanding of what could come to me and through me when I was not numb. I wanted to be receptive. This motivated me to want to eliminate and prevent blockages in my body, energetically, spiritually, and physically, because I like being a conduit. I wanted more of the connection to the Universe, and the learning about myself and humanity, and the ability to teach others. I wanted to stay present in my body. This was part of being present in the moment. Up until recently, I had viewed presence as mindfulness—for example, listening and not drifting to my to-do list or replaying something that happened yesterday that was bothering me. The definition of presence had expanded to include my physical body. I had developed a habit over many years of abandoning my body, not listening to what it told me, pushing through pain, working through exhaustion, and eating when I was hungry for something spiritual or emotional but not food. This new idea of being present with my body meant not watching TV or scrolling through my phone while I ate. It meant sitting with myself in the discomfort of physical hunger and being curious about where I felt it in my body, and what my self-talk was saying, and what triggered it. I explored intermittent fasting to deepen my understanding of my hunger and challenge old beliefs of food scarcity that hadn't been true for decades. It meant taking care of my physical needs as they arose, even if they felt inconvenient. It meant moving my body to help it process out the energy of things it had grown accustomed to shrink-wrapping and tucking away deep inside of me.

After being home for a while, my mind continued to reflect on the divine feminine and how that was an important part of my experience. I have been learning to embrace my own divine feminine, and the Universe provided so many opportunities for me to witness it in action. My tribe of female friends at home were all helping me get through my quarantine and assimilate back into my life at home. Filling my cup with examples of the divine feminine in action, they were heart-centered, wise, intuitive, compassionate, nurturing, collaborative, and creative. And, of note, it was almost entirely men who cared for me in person in Hulhumalé. I saw the divine feminine showing up in the young men who operated the hotel and provided comfort to me with things like fresh sheets and bug spray, and the man who helped me do my shopping at the market, and the dive boat manager who kindly checked in with me periodically so I would know I had not been forgotten, and the doctor who provided information and encouragement until I was cleared to board my plane home, and the restaurant owner who compassionately granted me the ability to use my credit card so I could have nourishment. These men, living in a culture that promoted masculine control and domination, also had a beautifully equipped feminine side that I was blessed to witness firsthand.

CONCLUSION

IN OUR FEAR OF OUR FEAR, we keep ourselves small, we settle, we hold ourselves back. We are often unable to access what is *for* us on the other side of the fear. Perhaps it is what we perceive to be on the other side that we are so afraid of. That was my situation as I faced the possibility of divorce. Being alone was what was on the other side of a divorce, and that was my Big Fear—not the divorce itself, but the aloneness afterward. We label the *catalyst* as the fear. Fear of heights is not accurate. Height can be a catalyst for falling, and we are actually afraid of the falling, not the height itself. Therefore, we choose to avoid the perceived fear of heights in order to feel safe from the actual fear of falling. We deprive ourselves of certain experiences, and of being fully present, when we avoid the things we fear will be catalysts to our Big Fears. I tried (and "succeeded") for many years to avoid the perceived fear of divorce in order to avoid the true fear of being alone. Ironically, I felt far more alone in those years of a marriage that was no longer working (as fear kept me from being my authentic expression of myself) than I did once I moved out and lived alone. There was freedom in that new "alone."

Lonely inside a relationship or free to be fully myself alone and enjoy my own company … easy choice now in hindsight.

Through experiencing our fears and actively seeking the gifts inside them, we let go of the things that are keeping us small or holding us back. We unveil our authentic self. It is like a rebirth, and we can feel vulnerable and raw and frail at first. We find compassion for ourselves and others in this space. We find our tribe, and community, and support—tangible and spiritual. We realize we survived that thing we were afraid of and that it is *beautiful* on the other side. From this perspective, we now understand the why, and we can become grateful for the very experience we had been terrified of.

HEIGHTS

by Janine Valentine

For most of my life,
Like many people I know,
I've had a fear of heights.
Although…
Fear doesn't quite define the sensations.
The word TERROR better describes
My internal state at elevations.
My body, paralyzed.
Barely breathing,
Heart palpitating,
My mind reeling.
Like a spider trapped
In her own web –
Holding myself back
From nourishment.

As if I cannot trust myself
Not to suddenly lose my balance
On this perfectly flat surface.
Or to let go
As if compelled
Into the void of space below —

Unaware my mind might be planning
A darkly secret crime of opportunity
Should I ever get near enough to the edge
Seizing the moment to brutally
Plummet me to my death.

Recently I made a discovery.
An "aha" moment that is
Perhaps the key to recovery.
The fear is not of being up high.
Being up high actually amplifies
Where the root of the fear lies.
This terror we name "fear of heights"
Is actually the fear of FALLING, right?

As if we cannot trust ourselves
Not to suddenly lose our balance
On this perfectly flat surface.
Or to let go
As if compelled
Into the void of space below —
Unaware our minds might be planning
A darkly secret crime of opportunity
Should we ever get near enough to the edge
Seizing the moment to brutally
Plummet us to our deaths.

Interestingly, this also applies
To a plethora of life's highs.
We work to be the best
Only to then fear being put to the test …
And FALLING.
Having our best bested.
Being replaced.
Imposter syndrome outed.
Being disgraced.
We fall from popularity.
We fall out of grace.
We fall out of favor.
We fall out of love.
The truth of this life
Is that if we reach heights
We potentially fall.

The fear of these falls
Holds us back from being outstanding.
Taking the lead.
Taking the leap.
Experiencing triumph.
Going first class.
Shattering that glass!
Overcoming.
Achieving success.
Being the best.
Going ALL IN.
Owning our skin.

I CAN trust myself
Even when I feel off balance.
My shadow side
Craves LIFE ... not death.
My survival instinct has been tested.
What if I were to lean over that edge
As if truly invested?
Seize the moment
To explore the space below
For patterns and lessons?
Heights bring perspective.
Our falls hold a message:

Let go and climb that mountain.
Achieve elevation!
Falling is not dying.
It's the prerequisite
For FLYING!

Sometimes when we are in the midst of something that scares us, we are not able (or not willing) to receive the message or insight that will come from the experience. The key is to know there *is* a message, and that it will come. I encourage you to look for it and listen when you are ready. During my quarantine experience, I was completely stripped down so I would be able to feel and hear my voice and my body and the Universe. God took away all the noise, the numbing, the distractions, the to-do lists, the comforts, the reliance, the codependence. These were all my avoidance tools, and there was no room for those there in that heightened state of being. Instead, what I found was all the collateral beauty inside the fear, loneliness, and grief. There will always be both light and shadow, calm and turbulence. These provide contrast. They are not opposites, but rather, intertwined parts of a whole, each necessary to the existence of the other, not as contradiction but rather as the full expression, the complete awareness and experience. Grief needs to be felt. Beauty needs to be witnessed. We all need to be fully seen, as the full spectrum of ourselves. How very much we miss by just not looking for it. It is not a matter of good or bad, easeful or challenging. There is room for both. They coexist. They harmonize, the energetic vibrations resonating like our collective voices in a yoga class, chanting om in unison. Our total experience of the full spectrum—from beauty and trust to fear and loss—are our own personal calls to prayer, washing over us before dawn.

We tend to negate or invalidate our feelings that are considered less desirable, like shame, fear, guilt, anger, frustration, loneliness, despair … this list goes on. This just discredits our own perception of ourselves, and frankly, is dishonest. Pushing these emotions down under the surface does not make them go away. They pop back up over and over until we deal with them, even if that is years later. They take hold in our physical bodies and cause all kinds of issues because the energy of those emotions must go somewhere, and it cannot leave us until we have acknowledged it, experienced it, blessed it, and released it.

During my quarantine weeks, I was intent on not allowing the fear, the anger at God, and the desperation to rise up and have a voice because it made me even more afraid that I might manifest *more* of that. I shoved all that down inside myself every time it rose up. The more I pushed it down, the more it popped up in another place. It was taking more of my time and energy than ever. After the night when I wrestled with God over this, I realized that allowing space for all my emotions validated the thing I was aware of … in this case, the fear of not making it home. That was a valid fear. It was okay that I was feeling that. It also introduced a new perspective that could *also* be true … in this case, I did indeed trust that I would get home. I did not have to reject my fear or try so hard to do the impossible—letting go of being afraid—in order to open up to the state of trust in my higher power, and I did not have to eliminate the possibility of having, and leaning into, that trust in order to validate or defend my current state of fear.

Here's the thing. The fear never went away. All the way until I got on that flight home, I was in fear. We move through and with fear. It is an unachievable goal to think we can reach a point when we just leave our fear sitting in an isolation cell somewhere while we go on without it. That belief leads us to denial of our fear, invalidation of it, and eventually, that game of Whack-a-Mole where it just explodes out of us over and over in any place it can.

Fear has ebbs and flows—times when it subsides or sinks beneath the surface and times it rages loud and clear. It is always present, just not always within our awareness. Sometimes we choose to face our fear, like if we decide to experience a zipline even though we are afraid of ~~heights~~ falling. Sometimes the Universe uses something we are afraid of to move us to the next level and makes it so big that we have no choice but to go through it—like losing a loved one, being diagnosed with a potentially terminal illness, being fired from a job, or being evicted from our home—and, as I experienced this time around, being left behind in a foreign country after testing positive for COVID-19.

Being unaware of our fear does not mean it does not exist. Fear took the entire journey with me. Fear sits on the couch behind me now as I write this book. Loss and change will continue to trigger fear. The difference is I am not letting it hold me back. I allow the fear space to express itself. I hold Fear by the hand with compassion, and together we move forward looking for Fear's quieter companions, Love and Beauty. They are always there as well.

When Fear speaks up, it is okay if we momentarily stop to listen. Our first reaction does not need to be slamming the door closed and hiding under the bed. There can be a conversation first. I have learned to invite my Fear to sit beside me for a chat. It rants and cries, repetitive and irrational at times. I listen and soothe, validate what might be true, and speak what is also true in response to its exaggerations. I ask questions that show there can be a way out without giving up or hiding or becoming small. Fear likes to say things like, "I am all alone," "I don't have any food or water," or "I can't leave this room."

The key is to remove its power. Fear no longer gets to have dominion over my life. It did for a very long time. With all my heart, I hope to lessen that for you. This is why I wrote this book. I do not want another person anywhere in this world to feel as though they need to make their life smaller because of fear. Please, live your life. The scary parts don't last that long. And I cannot stress enough that allowing the fear, and moving through it, is worth it.

Fear has purpose. It guides us to what is true so we can problem-solve, make choices that support our highest and best self, and survive. As an example, here are my responses to a couple of the fears that were presenting themselves to me in those first few hours of quarantine:

Yes, I feel alone, but the truth is that there are people here. I just don't know them yet, and we don't speak the same language. I do believe that humanity is overarchingly kind, and I can find someone who will help another human if I need to. I may be in quarantine, and my exposure to other humans must be limited, and what is also true is that I can share a smile from a safe distance and that will remind me that I am not alone. Also, although I have never met him, I have the phone number for a local doctor who knows my situation and will help me if I need it.

Yes, it is true that I do not have food or water at the moment, and that room service is no longer the solution I expected it to be. Yes, it does look like I will need to either break quarantine to source myself or risk being kicked out if I choose to tell one of the staff members here the truth in order to enlist his assistance. This fear has risks that must be weighed and is clearly triggering an avalanche of other fears. However, what is also true is that I am not going to die of dehydration or hunger. There are solutions, and though it may be hard, I am capable and I am sourced, even if I do not yet see how.

Writing this book was easy in that it just flowed out of me. Much of it was directly drawn from my journals. But it was also difficult. One of the hardest parts of writing this book was going back through all my WhatsApp conversations to include some of those texts verbatim, as well as to extract details and insights I may have forgotten or left out. I procrastinated on this piece of my writing process for a couple of months, and when I finally spent a weekend going through them I understood why I had been resistant. Returning to those text conversations put me right back there. It was the same thing when it came to reading the whole manuscript start to finish to add anything that felt like it was missing or needed more clarity. I felt a duality of conscious receptivity (openly and gratefully receiving guidance as I wrote) and unconscious resistance (a clenching against the openness required to write). Each time I revisited what I had written, my body was in trauma response. I got achy and developed a headache and even diarrhea. Sometimes I got dizzy or felt tightness in my chest like it was difficult to take in a deep enough breath. I cried again *every time*, at the hard parts and the happy parts. I felt it all as if it were still happening. This is the power of words. The emotions remain attached to them, just as they remain in our bodies. Another Reiki session revealed to me that it did not feel safe to me to revisit the experience, to engage with the emotions again. Fear had settled back into my sacral and root chakras, so I did the work to keep myself all the way open, knowing and trusting that I was indeed safe, and I continued writing.

I do not know if these words will carry their full weight of emotion for you as the reader, but my hope is that enough of it is conveyed in a way that is resonant and impactful for you to participate through my experience and glean some of the lessons for yourself without experiencing all the pain. As I read back through my manuscript, I self-soothed by reminding myself that I was no longer there. And yet, part of me *is* still there on my Warrior Bench in the Maldives, experiencing the fullness of duality. I remember that voice in my head saying to me on the beach that this time, it was not about what I took with me, but rather about what I left there.

Oh, yes. There was one more thing I was leaving behind that I didn't realize at the time. It turns out that part of me shall remain forever on that Warrior Bench, gathering truth from the Sea, speaking it into the sky overhead, and sending that patch of sky with love to all of us. I lean against Trust's shoulder and Fear stands nearby. We hold hands, the three of us, and walk along the beach continuing our conversations with the Sea.

ACKNOWLEDGMENTS

I AM SO GRATEFUL TO HAVE THE OPPORTUNITY to share my cathartic experience with you. I hope you find pieces of yourself along the way. You are the reason I wrote it all down. May you be well, may you be brave, may you be YOU.

As I reflect on all the so-called "little things" that people said or offered, these were never received as small gestures. There were so many things that others did for me during my quarantine and upon my return that I could not include them all in this book. There were friends who did distance energy healing (Judith) and Reiki (Stephanie) for me, and Tara sent regular recorded voice memos to me from the UK because her time zone wasn't as far off as that of my Colorado connections. Thanks to the myriad of prayer warriors and master manifesters all envisioning my safety and homecoming and checking in via WhatsApp. I am so blessed by the variety of ways that people provided help, courage, comfort, and encouragement to me along the way. We learn from receiving. I now have new ideas in my quiver of gifts that I can offer to others, thinking well beyond chicken soup and flowers.

I also extend my heartfelt eternal gratitude to:

My travel companions to the Maldives: Wendy, Jenny, Laura, Kevin, Julie, Robyn, Alex, Melinda, Liezel, Amy, and Chris.

The entire crew and staff of ScubaSpa Yang, with a special shout out to Max, Shifaau, Shahadat, and Jim, who all continued to check in on me until I was safely home.

My reluctant safe place during quarantine, Planktons Beach hotel, and the two young men who took care of me there, Sahin and Rubel. I don't know if they ever suspected or figured out that I was COVID-positive. If they did, they never once let on. (And if either of you are reading this, I am sincerely sorry that I was not able to be honest with you about my circumstances. I was scared, and I did my best to protect you, and I appreciate all you did for me immensely.)

The men who worked the counter and in the kitchen at The Chill Café, providing access to nourishment for me when I needed it most.

My shopping helper at the market ... I never did ask his name, which I regret. I was always stressed during my shopping excursions, self-conscious of my contagion, desperate to find things I could eat, and worried about my ability to carry it back to my room.

Dr. Usama and the technicians in both of his clinics, who helped me navigate the ever-changing rules, and while I was still bound by those rules, they still managed to convey their genuine care and concern for my mental and physical well-being.

My pet sitter, Robin, who graciously more than doubled her stay with my fur babies and sent me regular photos, updates, and texts of encouragement.

My longest (we don't like to say "oldest") best friend, Lois, who was unable to go on this vacation with us but showed up for me the whole time I was gone and well after my return. She is highly empathic and was the only one who openly cried with me rather than trying to be strong for me, which validated my own tears and made me feel so known and loved.

My family: Brittany and Austin (my adult children), Jane (the warrior's mom), Wendy (my beloved sister who was a lifeline for me throughout), Todd (my brother who held beliefs as truth when I could not), and Jenn (my sister-by-marriage, who also is the ridiculously talented graphic designer who created my book cover).

My assistants and faithful responders to the Bat Signal, Denice and Ali, and my clients who hung in there for nearly a month without me.

The members of my AWE tribe who were there vigilantly for me as resources, confidantes, healers, and encouragers: Cynthia, Jean, Kelly Grace, Stephanie, Karyn, Genevieve, Judith, Tara, Janice, Betsy, Melinda, Liezel, Lisa G., Pam, Mary Jo, Nadine, Deanne, Carie, Kathy, Angie, Karen, and Lisa H.

My energy healers: Christen (Reiki), who kept my chakras open and balanced while I wrote and invited my guides and angels into our sacred circle to help. Those sessions were instrumental in my understanding and processing of the experience. And Elena (ortho-bionomy), who helped restore my physical health as my body purged itself.

My early readers, who allowed me to practice the vulnerability of sharing my story in this way and gave me the courage to continue with their heartfelt feedback.

And the experts who came alongside me to help me get this book out into the world as the very best it could be, who are now part of my tribe for life: Jan Stapleman (proof editor, whose company—in another grand synchro-nicity of the Universe—is named Fearless Communications), Victoria Wolf (formatting and layout), Polly Letofsky (owner of My Word Publishing and my personal advisor, who found the perfect balance between being my cheerleader and telling me to "calm the fuck down" when I needed it most), and Bobby Haas (my editor extraordinaire, who was protective of my voice and knew exactly how to draw more out of me). I believe Bobby was divinely appointed to work with me—the alignment and energy as we worked together was otherworldly.

To all of you, I am You are We.

WITH LOVE, FROM JANINE

Go to www.janinevalentine.com/resources to
download a free PDF that includes:

QUESTIONS TO PONDER, JOURNAL, AND DISCUSS

Janine created questions for each chapter of the book,
perhaps to be used during discussion with your book club
or for your own journaling and introspection.

While you are on Janine's website, if you are in a book
club, click on the Book Clubs tab for information on
having her visit yours (in person or virtually)!

TOOLBOX

Janine offers a list of resources she regularly uses to help calm,
center, and ground herself. Grab a copy to experiment with,
and find what works for you. Build your own customized set
of tools to have close at hand when you need them.

*"In that dark, cavernous stomach, I used my tools to light a match.
And I kept that flame going. I lit my path home."*

—Janine Valentine